"Education Has Nothing
to Do with Theology"

Princeton Theological Monograph Series

Series Editor, K. C. Hanson

Recent volumes in the series

David A. Ackerman
Lo, I Tell You a Mystery

John A. Vissers
The Neo-Orthodox Theology of W. W. Bryden

Sam Hamstra, editor
The Reformed Pastor by John Williamson Nevin

Byron C. Bangert
Consenting to God and Nature

Stephen Finlan and Vladimir Kharlamov, editors
Theosis: Deification in Christian Theology

Richard Valantasis et al., editors
The Subjective Eye: Essays in Honor of Margaret Miles

Caryn Riswold
Coram Deo: Human Life in the Vision of God

Paul O. Ingram, editor
Constructing a Relational Cosmology

Mark A. Ellis, editor and translator
The Arminian Confession of 1621

"Education Has Nothing to Do with Theology"

James Michael Lee's Social Science Religious Instruction

EDWARD J. NEWELL

Pickwick *Publications*
An imprint of *Wipf and Stock Publishers*
199 West 8th Avenue • Eugene OR 97401

"EDUCATION HAS NOTHING TO
DO WITH THEOLOGY"
James Michael Lee's Social Science Religious Instruction
Princeton Theological Monograph Series 61

Copyright © 2006 Edward J. Newell. All rights reserved. Except for brief quotations in critical publications or reviews, no part of this book may be reproduced in any manner without prior written permission from the publisher. Write: Permissions, Wipf & Stock, 199 W. 8th Ave., Suite 3, Eugene, OR 97401.

ISBN: 1-59752-527-8

Cataloging-in-Publication data:

Newell, Edward J.
"Education has nothing to do with theology": James Michael Lee's social science religious instruction / Edward J. Newell.

Eugene, Ore.: Pickwick Publications, 2006
Princeton Theological Monograph Series 61

x + 120p.; 23 cm.

Includes bibliography

ISBN: 1-59752-527-8

1. Lee, James Michael. 2. Christian educators—United States. 3. Christian education—Philosophy. I. Title. II. Series.

BV1464 L4418 N4 2006

Manufactured in the U.S.A.

For Françoise Darcy-Bérubé

Contents

Acknowledgments / ix

Introduction / 1

1. James Michael Lee's Religious Instruction Theory / 11
2. Empiricism's Metaphysical Commitments / 36
3. The Theology of James Michael Lee / 70
4. Conclusions / 92

Bibliography / 111

Acknowledgements

Sincere thanks are due to everyone who helped me in this project. Thanks to Professor Mary Boys for her consistently constructive criticism. Thanks to scholars who took time to critique a chapter or two: Professors John Kuentzel, Michael Warren, Robert W. Pazmiño, and Harold W. Burgess. Thanks to Winnie Cameron, city librarian extraordinaire. Kind thanks are due to Dr. Anna Mary Burditt; her interest was expressed in editorial suggestions always given graciously. I would be remiss not to thank my parents, Floyd and Mary Newell; without their support the project would never have been. And my wife, Wanda, has been a rock through it all.

As always, faults and omissions are entirely to do with the author.

Introduction

James Michael Lee's lifework was a theory of religious instruction based on "social science." His claim was that religious instruction depends on the social sciences, not at all on theology.

The most prolific mainstream religious educator of his time, Lee was a professor of education who taught at the University of Notre Dame from 1962 to 1977, and afterwards at the University of Alabama at Birmingham. He authored or edited fourteen books and dozens of articles. As founder and publisher of Religious Education Press, he published leaders in the field as well as his own later work. His work includes texts on secondary education, seminary education, guidance, pluralism in education, and the sacramental character of teaching, but after a 1968 article on catechetics, Lee's concern was mainly for social science religious instruction.[1] The startling assertion was the thesis of his first major religious education work, *The Shape of Religious Instruction*, in 1971, and continued to be his burden up to 2000. The assertion that religious instruction is a mode of the social sciences was unmodified in a significant 1982 essay,[2] and was set forth again for a 2000 volume.[3]

By taking the strong position that he did, Lee gave Christian and religious educators an opportunity to clarify the theology-social science relationship. Current thinking about theology in relation to the social sciences should deeply affect the theory of religious education. Analyzing Lee will lead us to see that educational methodology is not neutral. His advocacy can show educators how commitments about God, the world, and the nature of being human affect any educational method. We begin to see that education always expresses an ontology, or a metaphysics.

---

[1] James Michael Lee, "Religious Education: What Is It?" *Discovery: A Forum for High School Religion Teachers* (March 1968) 1–3.

[2] Lee, "The Authentic Source of Religious Instruction," in *Religious Education and Theology*, ed. Norma H. Thompson (Birmingham, Ala.: Religious Education Press, 1982) 100–97.

[3] Lee, "Vision, Prophecy, and Forging the Future," in *Forging a Better Religious Education in the Third Millennium*, ed. James Michael Lee (Birmingham, Ala.: Religious Education Press, 2000) 243–67.

How theological claims relate to social scientific findings—a broad inquiry of its own—has been recognized as significant for religious education. Norma Thompson's 1982 edited volume, *Religious Education and Theology*, included essays by leading education theorists. Leading religious educators including Gabriel Moran and Randolph Crump Miller provided theoretical and historical analyses of the theology-religious education relationship, and Lee's proposal to displace theology's leading role ran to nearly a hundred pages. Surveys of the field such as Mary Boys's *Educating in Faith* (1989), Jack Seymour's *Mapping Christian Education* (1997), or Harold Burgess's *Models of Christian Education* (1995) make it clear that more than one understanding of the social sciences in religious education is possible. Lee's view is that the choice of theology or the social sciences for one's foundation is the most significant choice.[4]

Lee provides a great deal of writing for a study such as this one. Lee claims that his social science religious instruction theory is the only fully developed theory of religious instruction. His theory is most fully set forth in a trilogy: *The Shape of Religious Instruction* (1971), *The Flow of Religious Instruction* (1973), and *The Content of Religious Instruction* (1985). The three books set out a comprehensive theory of religious instruction. The trilogy has a prolegomenon justifying Lee's definitions and commitments (*Shape*); a theory of instruction (*Flow*); and a description of instruction by nine parameters—product, process, cognitive, affective, etc. (*Content*).

Lee supports his theory with vigorous polemics. Lee's view of theology in educational method is negative and his advocacy for the social sciences is entirely positive. He says that "social science" is the one true foundation of religious instruction. Lee's social sciences are a cluster of disciplines that he never portrays as sharing common ground with theology. He believes that a good future for religious instruction, the development of effective practice, is hinged on the profession accepting the pivotal role of empirical findings.

This study is a response to Lee's challenge to religious educators. It is the first full length study of social scientific religious instruction. He contended that empirical results should direct religious instruction. I argue that the social sciences are not basic to religious education. Rather, Lee's understanding of the social sciences rests on an implicit theology from which many educators differ. Thus, religious instruction should not be thought to depend on the social sciences. Religious educators instead

---

[4] *Harper's Encyclopedia of Religious Education*, s.v. "Social Science," gen. eds. I. V. Cully and K. B. Cully (New York: Harper & Row, 1990) 599. The article is signed by Lee.

need an employment of the social sciences consistent with their theological commitments.

Six Reasons to Read This Book

Religious education needs to move forward. But setting out a series of foundational proposals that in some way are all valid is simply inadequate. This indiscriminate approach is the way of Jack Seymour, and the same approach is employed by others.[5] Seymour sees more-or-less compatible paradigms within the field. But resolutions such as his fail to help a practitioner label what he or she is doing in ministry with any degree of precision. Educators need foundations for practice and reflection.

By contrast, Lee comes with a definite proposal. He advances one alternative—clearly, forcefully, polemically. Teasing Lee's religious instruction theory apart will not yield the one true key, the only solution. However, examining Lee proves to be a process of clarification that develops confidence for ministry. I mention six reasons why Lee is helpful.

Reason One: Lee challenges educators regarding methodology. By highlighting method, Lee effectively challenges educators to account for their own methods—or even, to disagree on the centrality of method as usually conceived. The more carefully methodological consideration is done, the more clearly educators can agree and disagree with each other. Explicit methodology can enable educators to learn from each other.

Reason Two: Lee's theorizing challenges educators to take a position on the relationship of theology to education. Theology's relation to the practice of educating is an almost inevitable investigation for all religious educators. Theology includes the meaning of being fully human, the goal of human life, and the nature of the ideal community. These are crucial matters for any educating that aims at more than minimal skill training. Lee clearly states his position on the theology-social science relationship. Educators will gain precision by taking ownership of their own conception of the relationship.

Reason Three: Lee challenges educators by highlighting quantitative measurement. To the question, "Is religious education quantitatively mea-

---

[5] For instance, Sara Little seems to opt for religion and education as "interactive" as her basic mode in a signed *Harper's Encyclopedia of Religious Education* article, but also identifies another methodological option as valid for a different circumstance. *Encyclopedia*, s.v. "Theology and Education," 654. Christian educator James Loder, accounting for "Theology and Psychology" in the *Dictionary of Pastoral Care and Counseling*, similarly concludes that "no single methodology will do the job satisfactorily," eds. C. Gifford, D. Perkins, et. al. (Nashville: Abingdon, 1990).

surable?," Lee answers "yes." Many proposals in current general education also assume that learning is measurable; for example, states or provinces mandate standard examinations as the main evaluation tool. If the practice is contentious in general education, then the measurability of religious education is certainly not less so. Can quantitative measurement be applied to faith, and if so, when?

Lee's emphasis on measurable goals poses a theological challenge. The ancient question of "works" in relation to faith surface again. How central is faith in Christian or religious education? What makes an action "Christian"? How does motive, drive, or compulsion, factor into an evaluation of behavior as "religious"? In Lee's preferred social-scientific terminology, can faith be entirely "operationalized"? I will show alternatives to Lee's position.

Reason Four: Lee's theorizing implicitly challenges educators to become clear on the ways in which their personal commitments work into their practice of Christian education. Lee's body of work makes a vivid case study in the way that philosophical, theological, and historical cultural factors shape educational paradigms. Uncovering the paradigmatic status of religious education is the distinctive contribution of Mary Boys to educational theorizing. Boys showed in *Educating in Faith* (1987) how a series of religious-educational expressions grew within theological understandings shaped by the ethos of an era. Religious educational theories are children both of broad theological positions and their times. Religious education proposals grow out of conceptualizations of God vis-à-vis culture, ideas about how God is revealed, what conversion is, what faith is, how a person learns, the nature of the ideal society, and a short list of others. The conditionality of education seen in Boys's historical analysis is sobering, and freeing. There is no once-and-for-all education theory. Educators must inquire about their educational sources, and must wrestle to attain consistency between deepest ideals and daily practice. Lee, by contrast, presents his process of educating as derived from authoritative social scientific sources alone. The movement of this study is to show the particular springs that support his theory. Lee's theory is well suited to a paradigm accounting.

Reason Five: Lee puts forward a version of education in a rationalist mode, but this is not education's only mode. Lee cites many authors, but he cites Robert Mager's *Preparing Instructional Objectives* repeatedly. Mager, and his educational kin Ralph Tyler, are rationalists who teach toward narrowly specified goals.[6] Lee presents a Tyler-rationale religion education. This is true even though Lee includes educational process as itself a kind of content and so modifies the "contents" or desired results of education.

Tyler's education is part of my own path as an educator, in this way: I first came to education as a business teacher, assigned by an overseas development agency to Papua New Guinea. My task: develop a business curriculum to accompany agricultural or mechanical skill training for early school-leavers. In that rural, traditional setting, business education seemed to mean training in clearly definable skills. If I could pass on specific skills, my trainees would be capable of employing agricultural or mechanical skills in their own small businesses. So I developed lessons for those skills. Subsequent reading brought me to Tyler and Mager's rationalistic understanding of education. They underlined my natural orientation to narrowly-specified goals. My vocational journey since the early business curriculum writing, however, has led me to see that teaching for faith differs from skill training. Looking at Lee will point towards a full-bodied education.

Reason Six: Lee's advocacy of social sciences in religious instruction is a starting point for investigating how the world as experienced relates to revelation or theology. For persons of faith, the world we see must be related to the world as God speaks of it. Lee's work is a case study in the ways that human observers inevitably project a worldview onto "data." The limitations of the straight-up empirical method become clear when it is seen that facts are facts only within a frame of reference. Worldview and data interact with each other. Understanding how immanent and transcendent reality interact should humble the sight-and-sense world. God's revelation must (and does) translate into the "real" world. Legitimate possibilities for empirical data become clearer for religious educators. Educators can exercise genuine wisdom in employing data.

I approach Lee with a set of lenses like his, yet different. Like Lee, I long to see my generation and the coming one live into the faith; there can be no doubt about the priority that Lee accords to the religious education lay "apostolate." In contrast to Lee, I am an ordained clergy person, not a lay person; Lee wears the lay designation with pride. I also come to Lee's works not as a Roman Catholic but as a Baptist. While I lack Lee's deep regard for sacrament or liturgy because of my own ecclesial commitment,

---

[6] Ralph W. Tyler, *Basic Principles of Curriculum and Instruction* (Chicago: University of Chicago Press, 1949); Robert F. Mager, *Preparing Instructional Objectives* (Palo Alto, Calif.: Fearon, 1962).

the church as an institution inspires passion like his. Our most significant difference, however, is theological. I am Reformed by training and inclination, with the characteristic Reformed desire to display God's gracious sovereignty over all areas of life.

Methodology

The methodology of this book is comparative and analytical. Working from primary works by Lee, and secondary sources, I analyze theoretical proposals from fields pertinent to religious education: theology, philosophy of science, and education. I am taking Lee's work as an educational paradigm, an educational expression of philosophical and theological commitments. Thus the method of the research is akin to the analysis of H. Richard Niebuhr in *Christ and Culture*[7] and applied to religious education by Mary Boys, first in *Biblical Interpretation in Religious Education*, later in *Educating in Faith*.[8] Another inspiration is analyses of intellectual history such as Alasdair MacIntyre's *Three Rival Views of Moral Inquiry*, in which MacIntyre analyzes three dominant intellectual positions in recent Western history—encyclopedist, genealogist, and Thomist.[9] He lays presuppositions bare. I hope to do the same for Lee's social science religious instruction. A third inspiration—my use of "paradigm" is an obvious clue—is Thomas Kuhn's *Structure of Scientific Revolutions*, where Kuhn presents fact and theory as a connected system, and replacement of dominant paradigms as not incremental but entire.[10]

Although Lee first set out his position more than three decades ago, a historical analysis is unnecessary. He continued to set forth his virtually unmodified thesis up to 2000. I examine Lee's proposal in perspectives from theology and philosophy of science published as recently as 2001, but also extending back to the early 1900s or before.

The focus of this book is on Lee's social science religious education, so the bibliography omits works that do not deal directly with his argument for social science religious instruction. For instance, articles on the distinctive vocation of lay persons do not appear.

---

[7] H. Richard Niebuhr, *Christ and Culture* (New York: Harper & Brothers, 1951).

[8] Mary C. Boys, *Biblical Interpretation in Religious Education* (Birmingham, Ala.: Religious Education Press, 1980); idem, *Educating in Faith: Maps and Visions* (Kansas City: Sheed & Ward, 1989).

[9] Alasdair MacIntyre, *Three Rival Versions of Moral Inquiry: Encyclopedia, Genealogy, and Tradition* (Notre Dame: University of Notre Dame Press, 1990).

[10] Thomas S. Kuhn, *The Structure of Scientific Revolutions*, 2d ed (Chicago: University of Chicago Press, 1970).

Synopsis

Chapter 1 profiles Lee's theory. Chapter 2 considers the nature of empirical data as seen by philosophers of science and theologians who set forth a revolutionary way of conceiving social sciences. Chapter 3 analyzes Lee's implicit theology, exposing what is problematic about his claim to have a macro-theory for religious education. My exposé shows that social science religious instruction is itself the product of a theological stance encompassing specific affirmations. Lee's educational theory is neither neutral, and nor, as claimed, able to serve as a "foundation" across differing theologies and religious claims. Lee's theory really reflects a particular theology. Lastly, Chapter 4 explores implications of the study. How can empirical educational research contribute to religious instruction?

Lee in a Nutshell

Lee's desire is that learners personally experience religion. Like John Dewey, Lee's educational starting-point is epistemology. Dewey claimed that all knowledge is from experience. Lee also starts by asking how students gain knowledge. Like Dewey, Lee says that the key to better learning is to focus on experience. Lee wants an education that aims not for facts but for personal appropriation—in this case, of religion. He wants a religious education with the accent on "religious." Students by experience are to acquire not just knowledge but "religion."

Lee's way forward is by specified goals. He wants religious instruction to target specified "behaviors," advocating a taxonomy like that of Benjamin Bloom's taxonomy of psychological and other findings to set an order of teaching tasks.

The problem with religious education is its backwardness. Religious education has failed to attend to the science of teaching and learning. Lee contrasts instruction with two other "areas" of religious education. Educational counseling and educational administration long ago professionalized by adopting scientific models; religious instruction lags on behind.

Lee traced religious education's inability to specify goals to faulty theory or methodology. Religious education practice should no longer be theologically based. Order of presentation is no longer to be derived from, say, logical considerations of systematic theology. Lee sees that dogmatic formulations provide little guidance for educators seeking to improve practice. The absence of benchmarks retards evaluation, unlike the apparent situation in general education. Because theology's directives to religious educators are nonspecific, there is little guidance to stimulate innovation. Religious educators apprpriate techniques without adequate theoretical reason. Lee wishes a social scientific foundation for religious education. Lee wants theology to retain a place in "product" contents but no place in "process" contents. Theology should have no role in structuring the religious instruction act; that is to say, theology should have no role in methodology.

The stated theology that fuels Lee is immanentism. Lee says explicitly that he is an immanentist. Lee's openness to secular instruction theory is because he perceives God at work everywhere, in all fields of knowledge and action. His understanding of God's revelation as an on-going stream makes possible an appropriation of learning by experience.

Critique in a Nutshell

Lee's question mark against dogmatics (propositional theology) in the director's chair of religious education is valid enough. Most theorists will concede that instructional procedure based solely on dogmatic formulations is inadequate. Dogmatics gives no direct means of evaluation. Dogmatics gives little direct help to the practice of teaching.

However, a foundation for theory and practice—the social sciences, theology, or a combination—rightly continues to be an issue in religious education literature. Philosophy of social science is, of course, a field in its own right. There, "social science" is more than one thing. Variants of sociology exist, not just its empirical form, and other social sciences have similar variation. Lee's preferred view attributes value-freedom to the social sciences, and splits verifiable empirical "facts" from values, with values assigned to a theology. Lee denied the pejorative label of "positivist" but the label has to be re-affixed. True, Lee states an awareness that observation and theory are entwined in making "facts," but he does not go far with it.

Methodology in the social sciences diverged dramatically between 1962 and 2000, Lee's timeframe. Social sciences developed alternates to the empiricist understanding of fact. Broadly, Thomas S. Kuhn's *Structure of Scientific Revolutions* undermined scientific claims to objective truth.[11] N. R. Hanson earlier showed observation to be "theory laden." W. V. Quine's 1956 article critiquing "dogmas of empiricism" had also raised serious questions.[12] In general, the climate since 1970 has been unfavorable

---

[11] Thomas S. Kuhn, *The Structure of Scientific Revolutions*, 2d ed. (Chicago: University of Chicago Press, 1970).

[12] W. V. Quine, "Two Dogmas of Empiricism," in *A Logical Point of View* (Cambridge:

to overarching frameworks. New understandings of "social science" have become evident as new variants have emerged. Theologians recognized that theological assumptions are inevitable in, for example, sociology, as far back as Ernst Troeltsch (1931). Since 1975, mainstream Christian theorists have doubted empiricist "neutrality" in the social sciences. I draw upon some of these theorists, including Gregory Baum, Don Browning, and John Milbank. Milbank, for one, demonstrated that the possibility of social "sciences" was generated by unstated theological or metaphysical assumptions. Such theologians see neutrality as impossible and unnuanced empiricism as naïve. "Theology versus the social sciences" is a false dichotomy in their view. The possibility of social theorizing that is aware of its theological assumptions has emerged more clearly than before.

Lee presents his variant of social science either as the only kind or as foundational for other variants. In contrast to social sciences which openly acknowledge metaphysical and ethical aspects, however, Lee's empirical social science is not frank about its metaphysical basis. Rather than being neutral, able to ride above varieties of theology-driven instruction, social science religious instruction is a product of Lee's theological stance.

Lee indeed works from theology, stated and unstated, as Françoise Darcy-Bérubé pointed out in 1978.[13] Lee's social science religious instruction proposal depends on his understandings of God's transcendence, revelation, and the image of humanity including faith in relation to action; the nature of sin; and conversion. Lee's position in the Niebuhr Christ-culture typology is not the same as other practitioners. Other understandings are possible.

This study shows Lee's theology. The display undermines his claim to have a macro-theory for religious education. The ability to specify his theology makes clear that, far from being generic or universal in scope, Lee's social science religious instruction theory expresses foundational commitments, and religious education proposals generally express foundational commitments. Not all educators need to share a theology, but those who propose a master theory need to show that the proposal does not depend on their own position. Lee's social science religious instruction is a problem for theologically committed educators because Lee's theology is not for all.

Harvard University Press, 1981) 20–46. <http://www.ditext.com/quine/quine.html>.

[13] Françoise Darcy-Bérubé, "The Challenge Ahead of Us," in *Foundations of Religious Education*, ed. Padraic O'Hare (New York: Paulist, 1978) 117.

Implications for Education

The social sciences are not properly foundational for education. They mediate philosophical-theological assumptions to the level of practice. Education theory arises from philosophical-theological assumptions within a cultural or historical setting. An example is the education theory of Dewey. So, if not the social sciences, what are the true methodological bases of religious education? Contrary to Lee's claim, the question is still at issue.

The social sciences will continue to play varied roles in religious education method, but appropriation of empirical findings must be critical. The point of Baum, Browning, and Milbank is that use of the social sciences has been uncritical. Appropriation of the social sciences must parallel the philosophical-theological starting point of the practitioner. It is essential to frankly acknowledge one's worldview and to see that all facts are such within a worldview. Disputes about "facts" are, at some level, disputes about rival worldviews. Ways that Christian educators use the social sciences must become open to scrutiny.

Greater methodological clarity should lead to religious educators better able to compare notes with each other. Some educators indeed work from a theological position similar to that of James Michael Lee. Practical theologians such as Johannes Van der Ven continue to advance positivistic proposals. While Lee's (and Van der Ven's) immanentism is not accepted by all religious educators, some do understand God's working in the world in that way and in immanentist fashion could use social scientific findings unmodified. The existence of such theorists points to a continuing pluralism in religious education. Mapping methodological variance can only improve practice.

Missing in religious education is a link between theology and Christian practice. Religious education's need is an ability to move understandings of God, humanity, the church, society, into consistent practices. Links between education and Christian anthropology have become visible. A consistent understanding of humanness must be employed in religious education now that there is better understanding of the theology-social science relationship. Assumptions about the nature of persons, the church, or society—now seen as inherent in the social sciences—may no longer be taken over uncritically.

1

James Michael Lee's Religious Instruction Theory

JAMES Michael Lee claims that religious instruction should be founded not on theology but on empirical data. Lee's alternative wishes to employ empirically verified methods for specifiable religious behaviors. First, I profile his proposal for a social science religious instruction; then, we see contemporary peer reactions.

Theology is the traditional foundation of religious education, both Catholic and Protestant. Theologians like Augustine, and even earlier leaders, wrote catechisms. The tradition of catechesis revived at the Reformation, when Martin Luther leveraged new technology—the printing press—to disseminate Protestant doctrine through both comprehensive and family-sized, "Large" and "Small," catechisms (1529). Protestant catechesis was met by the counter-reformation catechisms of Peter Cansius (1554–1558) and the Roman Catechism (1566).[1] The Roman Catholic expression in the U.S. continued in the Baltimore Catechism (1885, 1941). Theology-derived catechesis continued to emerge in the twentieth century, including Josef Jungmann's salvation-historical catechetics (1936), and the official *Catechism of the Catholic Church* (trans. 1994). The Protestant mainstream-Episcopalians and Presbyterians at any rate—continued catechetical instruction in confirmation classes until the mid-twentieth century. Protestant evangelicals had an early catechetical phase, but after the 1830s avowed an a-theological, solely biblical, foundation for vehicles such as the Sunday School.[2]

---

[1] *Evangelical Dictionary of Christian Education*, s.v. "Catechism," ed. Michael J. Anthony (Grand Rapids: Baker, 2001).

[2] James C. Wilhoit, "The Bible Goes to Sunday School: An Historical Response to Pluralism," *Religious Education* 82 (1987) 390–404; Mary Jo Osterman, "The Two Hundred Year Struggle for Protestant Religious Education Curriculum Theory," *Religious Education*, 75 (1980) 535.

The Genesis of Social Science Religious Instruction

Lee is remarkably consistent. His position did not change from his first articles on religious education.[3] Lee developed a social scientific theory of instruction in his very first book, a 1963 textbook on Catholic secondary school education.[4] The elaboration of a social scientific Catholic education continued in *Seminary Education in a Time of Change* (1965), and *Guidance and Counseling in Schools* (1966). He used empirical results to raise questions about church-specific education.[5] Lee's work through the 1960s seeks to clarify the purpose of a Catholic school system that appeared to merely duplicate public education. For instance, he made a bold and widely noticed suggestion that Catholic elementary schools be eliminated for lack of empirically demonstrated effectiveness toward their stated goal of religious inculcation. Lee's first article on religious education appeared in a high school teacher's magazine in 1968,[6] but he had championed social scientific schooling for some time.

Lee's article put forward his model of religious education. The 1968 model is entirely consistent with later ones. There, Lee specifies that he is dealing not with religious education in general but with religious instruction. Instruction is a category within education. He argues for a distinction between religion teaching and theology, saying that to teach theology is not necessarily to make the student religious. Lee argues for the primacy of affective goals in teaching; he advocates the ultimate goal of charity or love in the learner; wishes a process approach to the task of teaching; and demands awareness of not just the teacher but all environmental factors. Similar features reappeared up to the most recent presentation.[7] In 1968

---

[3] As Kevin Coughlin noted in "Religious Education in Everyday Life" (PhD diss., Graduate Theological Union, 1981) 128.

[4] Lee, *Principles and Methods of Secondary Education* (New York: McGraw-Hill, 1963). See Lee, "To Basically Change Fundamental Theory and Practice," in *Modern Masters of Religious Education,* ed. Marlene Mayr (Birmingham, Ala.: Religious Education Press, 1983) 282.

[5] James Michael Lee, *The Purpose of Catholic Schooling* (Washington, D.C. and Dayton, Ohio: National Catholic Education Association and Pflaum, 1968).

[6] Lee, "Religious Education: What Is It?," *Discovery: A Forum for High School Religion Teachers* (March 1968) 1–3.

[7] Lee, "Vision, Prophecy, and Forging the Future," in *Forging a Better Religious Education in the Third Millennium,* ed. J. M. Lee (Birmingham, Ala.: Religious Education Press, 2000) 243–67.

in contrast to the "traditional" or theological approach, he called his package the "pedagogical" approach to catechetics.[8]

Lee's arguments were directed to a field showing signs of change. The reigning approach in 1960s Catholic religious education was the catechetics of Josef Jungmann and Johannes Hofinger. By the early years of the decade their salvation-historical catechetics had swept before it the long-established Baltimore catechism.[9] But by the late 1960s the catechetical journal *The Living Light* had published articles that questioned aims and methods of the newer catechesis.[10] Introducing three articles for *Today's Catholic Teacher* in 1969 Lee wrote, "It hardly comes as a surprise to indicate that the field of religious education is currently in a state of confusion and bewilderment."[11] Lee was in a growing chorus of critics.

Change was the mode of the 1960s, of course. Change in the Catholic church was defined when the documents of the Second Vatican Council (1962–65) were published in 1966, though newspapers had reported conciliar discussions. One affirmation was the potential of the social sciences. The Council directed that "sufficient use should be made, not only of theological principles, but also of the findings of secular sciences, especially psychology and sociology: in this way the faithful will be brought to a purer and more mature living of the faith."[12] No doubt the fathers were underlining a trend already present. But the declaration was part of an official opening of the church to the world and worldly knowledge. Lee's religious education proposal was part of the growing Catholic openness to the social sciences.

---

[8] Lee, "Religious Education: What Is It?" Part of the *Discovery* article reappeared in Lee, "The New Style of Catechetics in the USA," *Herder Correspondence* 5.5 (1968) 141–45.

[9] Boys, *Biblical Interpretation in Religious Education*, 231.

[10] Gabriel Moran, "The Future of Catechetics," *Living Light* 5.2 (1968) 6–22; Mary Perkins Ryan, "The Identity Crisis of Religious Educators," *Living Light* 5.4 (1968) 6–18.

[11] Lee, "The Third Strategy: A Behavioral Approach to Religious Education" in *Today's Catholic Teacher* (September, 1969) 10–12, 41–47. See also parallel in Lee, "To Basically Change Fundamental Theory and Practice," 296.

[12] "Gaudium et Spes," in *Vatican Council II: Constitutions, Decrees, Declarations,* ed. Austin Cannery (1975; reprint, Northport, N.Y.: Costello, 1996) No. 62. The statement is directed to pastoral care, but implicitly approves the social sciences for all ecclesial reflection.

Social Science Religious Instruction: Characteristics

Lee suggests that the educator must start, not with the content to be conveyed, as theology would tend to start, but with the learner.[13] The social scientific educator will have a new ability to specify definite goals because the learner's location will be charted from empirical science. Effective methods must be confirmed by empirical rigor too. Methods of instruction will no longer be prescribed by theology.[14]

Although he limits his concern specifically to instruction, Lee has a broad idea of instruction. In social science religious instruction all educational variables need to be recognized. Teacher centeredness was a feature of theologically driven religious education, but the social sciences prove that learning occurs from the whole environment.[15] Lee prefers the broader "facilitator" to "teacher."[16] Because he recognizes that learning occurs in the whole environment of the classroom, teaching theory is a subset of overall learning theory. Teaching must be seen as the structuring of all educational variables. A social scientific basis enables manipulation of all variables for desired results.[17]

Social science religious instruction was to be goal oriented, first of all. All education is necessarily oriented to some outcome; after all, a goal of some sort must be the reason for educating. But Lee is distinguished by the specificity of his goal. Lee wants religious education to produce, simply, religion, and there is a common-sense ring to his goal. To follow him precisely, the result of religious instruction is to be lived religion,

---

[13] Lee, "Toward a New Era: A Blueprint for Positive Action," in *The Religious Education We Need: Toward The Renewal Of Christian Education,* ed. J. M. Lee (Mishawaka, Ind.: Religious Education Press, 1977) 123.

[14] Lee, "Religious Instruction and Religious Experience," in *Handbook of Religious Experience,* ed. Ralph W. Hood (Birmingham, Ala.: Religious Education Press, 1995) 539–40.

[15] Lee, *The Shape of Religious Education: A Social Science Approach* (Dayton, Ohio: Pflaum 1971) 59, 217, 229, 239; Lee, "The Teaching of Religion," in *Toward a Future for Religious Education,* eds. Lee and Patrick C. Rooney (Dayton, Ohio: Pflaum, 1970) 92; Lee, "Toward a New Era," 131; Lee, *The Flow of Religious Instruction: A Social Science Approach* (Mishawaka, Ind.: Religious Education Press, 1973) 218, 237; Lee, "Behavioral Objectives in Religious Education," *Living Light* 7.4 (1970) 19; Lee, "Toward a Dialogue in Religious Instruction," *Living Light* 8.1 (1971) 118.

[16] Lee, *Shape,* 59; *Flow,* 210. Also 199, 242, 245; "Behavioral Objectives in Religious Education," 14; "Authentic Source," 127–28.

[17] Lee, *Shape,* 50, 74, 182, 187, 208; *Flow,* 41, 206; "Religious Instruction and Religious Experience," 542.

spirituality, what was traditionally called piety. Lee desires specifiable religious behaviors:

> [R]eligious instruction has as its central task the modification of the learner's inner and overt behaviors, the modification of his product and process behaviors, the modification of his cognitive and affective behaviors, and the modification of his lifestyle as he acts himself out in everyday living.[18]

Lee wants more than visible behaviors from his instruction, certainly. He includes inward belief as a "cognitive" behavior. He says that he uses "behavior" as a social science technical term,[19] and his breadth of meaning is evident from the quotation above. He says that the behaviors cannot be taught in isolation from the learner's self-system[20] and that doctrine, for instance, has to be "inserted into the learner's experience."[21] He specifies that the outcomes in proper order are lifestyle outcomes, affective outcomes and cognitive outcomes.[22] Lee therefore maintains a link with non-verifiable behavior change.

However, Lee is most concerned with outward religious behaviors. Outward behaviors are the behaviors that are testable and verifiable. Lee says, "To make the religion lesson effective, the goals of the learning experience should be expressed in terms of specific behaviors."[23] Again, "[o]perationalizing of an educational objective specifies the type of learning experience in performance terms, and hence is crucial to facilitate optimally the realization of the desired learning outcomes."[24] Since lifestyle outcomes are the empirically testable outcomes, outward religious behavior is the outcome that counts.

Lee's orientation to specific performance goals leads to a basic issue with theology-founded religious education. Lee sees that educators who rely on theology find it hard or impossible to develop clear teaching goals. "Lack of operationalizing is a major contributory cause of ineffective and

---

[18] Lee, *Shape*, 56–57.

[19] Ibid., 56; Lee, "Facilitating Growth in Faith through Religious Instruction," in *Handbook of Faith*, ed. J. M. Lee (Birmingham, Ala.: Religious Education Press, 1990) 270.

[20] Lee, *Shape*, 62.

[21] Ibid., 18.

[22] Lee, "Behavioral Objectives in Religious Education," 13; Lee, "Toward a New Era," 116, 126.

[23] Lee, "Behavioral Objectives in Religious Education," 15.

[24] Lee, *Shape*, 74; see also 188–89; *Flow*, 23, 55, 192, 276; "Toward a New Era," 126; "Facilitating Growth in Faith," 268.

fuzzy religion teaching . . . desired learning outcomes are laudable enough but they are terribly vague."[25]

Lee sharply distinguishes theology from religion. In a list of ten points in a 1976 manifesto for renewed religious education, item number one is the familiar "doable performance objectives"; item three is the emancipation of religious education from theology as "ontologically distinct."[26] Lee therefore wants a method of religious education that is theology-free. Theology may form a portion of the taught "material" or the "product contents" of religious education,[27] but theology has nothing to do with method, the considered process of educating religiously.

The first reason to liberate religious education from theology is for the sake of religion. The goal of religious education is to transmit religion, and theological knowledge will not yield personally appropriated religion. Taking only theological considerations into account is inappropriate for the educator who is striving for personal religiosity.

The second reason for separating religious instruction from theology, closely linked to the first, is that Lee's religion cannot be fully set forth in a theological account. Theology is just one perspective by which to view religious reality; other, equally valid, standpoints are available. Furthermore, theological considerations are inconsistent with the process of religious educating. Theology is cognitive, propositional, speculative, based on revelation, partial. Religion as a whole is experiential, a whole-life affair, a lived reality.[28] Religious knowledge is but one of five dimensions of religiosity—the intellectual dimension. Besides the intellectual dimension are the ideological dimension of religious belief, the ritualistic dimension of practice, the experiential dimension of feeling, and the consequential dimension of religious effects.[29]

A third reason for separating religious instruction from theology, linked to the first two, is in the nature of instructing. Instructing is a practical area of human endeavor, an art-science.[30] Theology, being cognition, has nothing to do with instructional practice. Religious instruction

---

[25] Lee, "Behavioral Objectives in Religious Education," 15; *Flow*, 218.

[26] Lee, "Roman Catholic Religious Education," in *Foundations for Religious Education in an Era of Change*, ed. Marvin J. Taylor (Nashville: Abingdon Press, 1976) 255–56.

[27] Lee, *Flow*, 22 ; *The Content of Religious Instruction* (Birmingham, Ala.: Religious Education Press, 1985) 8.

[28] Lee, "CCD Renewal," in *Renewing the Sunday School and the CCD*, ed. D. Campbell Wyckoff (Birmingham, Ala.: Religious Education Press, 1986) 222; *Content*, 39.

[29] Lee, *Shape*, 10.

[30] Lee, "The Third Strategy," *Today's Catholic Teacher* (September 1969) 10; *Flow*, 216.

thus operates on a different plane of reality than theology. In Lee's words, "Religious instruction enjoys ontic autonomy."[31] He writes further, "[i]n the term 'religious instruction' the word 'instruction' is the noun not only grammatically but ontically, and hence properly situates the word 'religious' as its qualifying adjective."[32] Theology is thus out of its place in trying to direct the "how" of religious instruction.

Religious instruction is for achieving the desired result, "religion." Lee wishes to be more specific than "education" allows. His preference for "instruction" reflects his background in general education, where education is sometimes departmentalized into instruction, guidance, and administration. The term "instruction" also serves to specify intentional education or deliberate teaching, not learning that is incidental, or accidental. Education may be gained unintentionally from an institution, the media, or the physical environment in general.[33] Wide-angle views of education are well recognized in religious education; educators of the past forty years have become aware of the multiplicity of factors that go into the formation of religious persons.[34] Lee is well-aware that religious formation develops out of a wide set of factors, and specifies intentional instruction as his concern, a controllable subset of religious education.[35] Lee wishes to focus on the "teaching-learning act."[36] Principally, he sees himself as a teaching-learning specialist.

For Lee, learning of all kinds is the same.[37] Learning is learning.

---

[31] Lee, "Authentic Source," 175; *Flow,* 17.

[32] Lee, "Religious Instruction and Religious Experience," 542; *Shape,* 183; *Harper's Encyclopedia of Religious Education,* s.v. "Social Science," gen. eds. Iris V. Cully and Kendig B. Cully (New York: Harper & Row 1990).

[33] Lee, *Shape,* 229; "Vision, Prophecy, and Forging the Future," 243; "Key Issues in the Development of a Workable Foundation for Religious Instruction," in *Foundations of Religious Education,* ed. Padraic O'Hare (New York: Paulist, 1978) 41; "Religious Education and the Bible: A Religious Educationist's View," in *Biblical Themes in Religious Education,* ed. Joseph S. Marino (Birmingham, Ala.: Religious Education Press, 1983) 2.

[34] Educators who write from a wide angled view of education include C. Ellis Nelson, John Westerhoff, Lawrence Richards, and Michael Warren; for comment see Edward Farley, "Can Church Education be Theological Education?" in *Theological Perspectives on Christian Formation,* eds. Jeff Astley, Leslie J. Francis, and Colin Crowder (Grand Rapids: Eerdmans, 1996) 31–44.

[35] Lee, *Shape,* 7.

[36] Ibid., 217; *Flow,* 8; Harold W. Burgess, *An Invitation to Religious Education* (Mishawaka, Indiana: Religious Education Press, 1975) 15.

[37] Lee, *Flow,* 202.

> There are no specifically labelled "Christian teaching processes." Nor does the [B]ible offer a model for a modern school or the organization of a religious education program . . . Attempts to create "Christian dentistry" or "Christian farming" and the like are no more ridiculous and unchristian than efforts to create "Christian teaching-learning process."[38]

Lee notes that Ronald Goldman's "highly significant" 1964 study of children and religious learning "concluded that 'religious thinking employs the same modes and methods of thinking applied to other fields.'"[39]

That religious and secular learning are the same is a core attribute of social science religious instruction. Setting out his distinctives for survey articles, both Jack Seymour and Harley Atkinson write first that Lee sees no difference between religious learning and any other type of learning.[40] Religious education is a subset of general education.[41] "At bottom, what the social-science approach to religious instruction does is to radicate it in the teaching-learning process. By this I mean that the central task of religious instruction becomes the conscious and deliber-ative facilitation of specified behavioral goals."[42]

What of theological material when it is, in Lee's terms, "substantive contents"? Theology employed in religious education becomes something different. In the religious instruction act, theology is changed into a new nature so the learner can absorb it into his or her self-system. Lee describes the change as similar to the compounding of a chemical, making one new substance from two. Religious instruction is an activity which "reconciles, brings to wholeness"—a "mediatorial" activity.[43] The phrasing suggests a change of nature. Lee says elsewhere,

> [I]f sacramental theory is incorporated within the framework of personality theory, and allowed free rein to interact with the various facts and laws inherent in personality theory, then religious in-

---

[38] Lee, *Shape*, 292, c.f. 208; parallel statement in "Authentic Source," 125–26.

[39] Lee, *Flow*, 60, 124.

[40] Harley Atkinson, s.v. "Lee, James Michael," in *Evangelical Dictionary of Christian Education*, ed. Michael J. Anthony (Grand Rapids: Baker Academic, 2001) 423; and Jack L. Seymour, "Contemporary Approaches to Christian Education," *Chicago Theological Seminary Register* 69 (Spring 1979) 1–10, reprinted in *Theological Perspectives on Christian Formation*, 3–13.

[41] Lee, "Authentic Source," 177; "Religious Instruction and Religious Experience, " 542.

[42] Lee, *Shape*, 217, c.f. 2.

[43] Lee, "Authentic Source," 172.

struction has achieved [a] congenial fruitful working relationship between theology and social science. . . .[44]

I return below to Lee's theological affirmations.

The Heart of Social Science Religious Instruction

It is no exaggeration to say that the heart of Lee's social science religious instruction is empirical observation. He holds observation in the highest regard.

> Social science is characterized by close adherence to observable data so that whatever conclusion is reached from the investigation follows naturally from the observable procedure rather than from sources which are speculatively authoritative, that is, not subject to empirical control. The formulation of laws and theories is based on empirically discovered data, and indeed these laws and theories are verified as far as possible on empirical grounds.[45]

The confidence flowing from empirical findings could not be more different than the confidence engendered by theology:

> [in theology-founded religious education] it has been inevitable that ideology should pass for theory in the absence of *empirical facts*. It has typically been upon ideology and not upon *hard data* as to how the teaching-learning of religion actually takes place, that religion curricula . . . were devised . . . Ideology is no substitute for hard data. Actually, ideology is counterfeit theory which, on account of inadequate foundations, soon tends to become verbal formulae and slogans that render *genuine theorizing as well as empirical verification* . . . *impossible*.[46]

Theology contrasts with "hard data"[47] and "genuine theorizing." Involving theology militates against certainty.[48] Lee states,

> . . . the extremely sharp divergence on the part of theological scientists as to their conclusions surely indicates a serious problem in terms of verification . . . [and] has serious implications for the no-

---

[44] Lee, *Shape*, 245.
[45] Ibid., 136; *Flow*, 196; "Vision, Prophecy, and Forging the Future," 266.
[46] Lee, *Shape*, 268; "Social Science," 599, emphasis mine.
[47] See also Lee, *Flow*, 196.
[48] Lee, *Shape*, 125–26.

> tion and strength and quality of verification in theological science, and indeed for the validity of theology as a science.[49]

In other words, deriving solid empirical knowledge from theology is impossible.

On the other hand, research uncovers facts.[50] The social sciences are about facts. Empirical research verifies facts. "Social science is characterized by close adherence to observable data . . . empirically discovered and verified data."[51] Again, "[d]uring each step of the investigation, from the systematic observation through the gathering of findings down to the formulation of conclusions, the social scientist is bound to follow the data, no matter how they fall."[52] A fact is a fact. "Facts simply are: they have no meaning and significance in and of themselves."[53]

Lee's confidence in observation flows into a definite understanding of what a theory is. Theory takes shape from the solid building blocks of facts.[54] "Without theory, reality would be personally meaningless and without . . . significance."[55] The one who makes theory from facts is making coherence, order, and meaning.

For Lee, then, advance in theory is the precondition to advance in religious education. "[T]he most practical thing in the world is a good theory . . . because theory . . . predicts which practices will tend to work in a given situation and which ones will tend to fail."[56] The problem of religious education is largely a problem of unaccounted-for practice.

> I firmly believe that one major cause for the relative inefficacy of much of contemporary religious instruction lies in the fact that most religion teachers hold one theory of religious instruction while at the same time . . . utilize pedagogical practices drawn from another highly-conflicting theory.[57]

---

[49] Ibid., 126.

[50] Lee, *Flow*, 196.

[51] Lee, *Shape*, 136.

[52] Ibid., 140.

[53] Lee, "Authentic Source," 117.

[54] Lee, *Shape*, 158; "Toward a New Era," 120; "To Basically Change Fundamental Theory and Practice," 296, 299; "Authentic Source," 123.

[55] Lee, "Authentic Source," 117.

[56] Ibid., 118–19; *Flow*, 26, 27, 39, 41, 42, 149.

[57] Lee, *Flow*, 27.

Lee indeed presents social science religious instruction as a master theory of religious instruction, a macrotheory that is "an overall and global form of theory into which are inserted theories and sub-theories of lesser scope."[58]

Taking in all forms of instruction, only religious instruction has not made the move to a scientific basis.[59] By comparison to guidance counseling or church administration, only religious education has yet to escape theological imperialism.[60] For instance, "When religious counseling became a branch of psychology, the dawn of a great new age in helping relationships was ushered in."[61] Theoretical advance has meant practical advance for other related areas. Religious instruction is a holdout.

The taproot of Lee's advocacy could be his respect for empirical experience over apparently arbitrary theory. In a 1983 autobiographical article Lee reflects on his 1954–1958 experience as a teacher in a public high school. "[T]heology utterly failed to directly generate or explain effective pedagogical practice." Even more strongly, "[T]he theological worldview was actually hindering me from teaching effectively . . . [it was] impeding me from searching for fruitful theoretical and empirical sources on which to base my day-to-day pedagogical activities."[62]

Lee understands the social sciences to be as reliable as physical sciences.[63] While he allows in a 1990 encyclopedia article, "Objectivity in social science is not the same as objectivity in philosophical science," the concession proves not to weaken social science objectivity: "[R]esearch data from both the social sciences and the physical sciences indicate that philosophical objectivity is not attainable by human beings."[64] It remains true that "[b]y use of carefully constructed methodological controls, social science can free itself from the inevitable tilt of the personal subjective judgment of researcher and so can attain a more or less objective approxi-

---

[58] Lee, "To Basically Change Fundamental Theory and Practice," 296; "Vision, Prophecy, and Forging the Future," 261.

[59] Lee, "Authentic Source," 142, 286.

[60] Lee, *Shape*, 242. It may not be especially significant that Lee selected 'guidance' and 'administration' with 'instruction' to represent the practical domains of the ecclesia, but it does seem a natural expression of a formal, structured conception of education and church.

[61] Lee, *Shape*, 242.

[62] Lee, "To Basically Change Fundamental Theory and Practice," 279.

[63] Lee, *Shape*, 239.

[64] Lee, "Social Science," 599.

mation of the personal and/or social phenomenon under investigation."[65] In comparison with "philosophical objectivity" the objectivity of physical science and social science are weaker, but, crucially, similar.

Lee's education theory includes progressive elements. Lee wishes the learners to assist in setting forth goals.[66] A living laboratory of religion is the way to most effectively educate, not lectures.[67] Lee wants a religious education within the tradition of general education's progressive school. To Lee this is an education already validated; empirical data have verified the theories of educators like John Dewey. While Lee is against teacher-centered maximum control approaches, he also wants definite results.

In summary, the great benefit of social science religious instruction is that educators attain a position from which they are able to employ a genuine method toward specified goals. Theology-based religious education sets goals but these are vague. Nor does theology have the technical resources to achieve its goals. Through social scientific findings, immanent goals can be specified, and immanent means are at hand to achieve them. The means of achieving the goals are empirically verified teaching techniques. Religious instruction needs now a taxonomy like Bloom's, et al., for general education—a definite series of sub-goals toward the desired religious product.[68] Religious educators must move from the ineffable world to the empirical world.

Lee and Theology

Lee's educational method is grounded on a particular understanding of how God is at work in the physical world. Lee is frank about this key pin of his theorizing; he devotes a chapter in the trilogy's first volume to his immanentist foundation. Lee contrasts his stance with that of "transcendentists" or "transcendists."[69] Lee's God works not "out of the sky," but immanently, through the created order. Transcendists in religious education are said to expect God to act directly on the learners, without employing human agents or "means." Lee suspects that "theologically-based learning

---

[65] Ibid.
[66] Lee "Behavioral Objectives in Religious Education," 17–18.
[67] Lee, *Shape*, 85.
[68] Lee, *Content*, 166.
[69] Lee, "Toward a Dialogue in Religious Instruction," 117; "Religious Education and the Catholic University," *Notre Dame Journal of Education* 4 (1973) 281.

theory is constructed on a defective theology of the nature and relationship of the natural and supernatural."[70]

> [A] teacher will teach a lesson quite differently if he views teaching as simply opening the pedagogical windows to let the Spirit blow where he wills (John 3:8), or, on the other hand, as purposeful behavior in which the teacher and other environmental variables exert predictable influences on the learner.[71]

Lee believes that religious instruction has been "bungled for centuries" because the church has "over-supernaturalized" nature, reflected in "over-theologized" religious instruction.[72] A wider gulf than necessary has been created.[73] Immanence and transcendence have been too far separated:

> It is unchristian to attempt to "baptize" a reality by trying to introject a labelled religious element into a sphere in which religion exists according to the mode of the reality rather than according to the mode of theology or of ecclesiastical activities. . . . Effective religious instruction first recognises and then actualizes the intimate inseparable structural relation between the natural and the supernatural.[74]

So "the surest way to bring a theory of religious instruction to those heights of humanity and divinity of which it is capable is to make it as scientific as possible."[75] Lee forces a choice between God's immanence and transcendence, opting for immanence. " . . . [A]lways present in every human act [are] both the immanent and the transcendent conditions. But from the standpoint of religious instruction, it is the immanent that is of crucial importance."[76]

---

[70] Lee, *Flow*, 47. Ian Knox states that a transcendist social science religious instruction is possible; the implication flows logically from Lee's assertion that social science religious instruction can accommodate any theological position. Knox's citation, though, does not confirm that Lee himself contemplates a transcendist social science religious instruction. Knox, *Above or Within*, 92, nn. 41, 42.

[71] Lee, *Flow*, 42.

[72] Lee, *Shape*, 228.

[73] An early statement is Lee, *Principles and Methods of Secondary Education*, 61–62.

[74] Lee, *Shape*, 292.

[75] Lee, *Flow*, 150.

[76] Lee, "Prediction in Religious Education," *Living Light* 9.2 (1972) 43.

Like the social science instruction theory itself, Lee's prioritizing of immanence goes back some time. He advocated for immanence in his first work, *Principles and Methods of Secondary Education*.[77]

Lee's immanentism is upheld by three considerations. The first support is a particular understanding of God's incarnation in Jesus Christ. To Lee, the event of incarnation transformed creation. After the advent of Christ, divine action is now human action. "Through the Incarnation, the supernatural and the natural were joined in one person, inseparable."[78] Something radical, even cosmic, occurred in the event of incarnation. Perhaps not surprisingly, Lee relies on evolutionary theologian Teilhard de Chardin alongside less controversial writers for authoritative support.[79]

The second support to the immanence substructure is an understanding of natural law. Lee says that "natural law" is one of "two major touchstones" of his theorizing (the other is "common sense").[80] His understanding of natural law is refined beyond the pre-Vatican II formula, St. Thomas Aquinas's two-tier schema of nature and grace:

> The development of a sophisticated theology of grace is the key to a valid explanation of natural-supernatural reality. It is not really accurate to assert that grace builds on nature, as the standard formulation states . . . grace suffuses nature.[81]

Unlike Aquinas's grace, Lee's grace does not stand above nature but is inherent throughout nature.[82] Lee takes the "sophisticated theology of grace" from theologians including Karl Rahner, Paul Tillich, Yves Congar, and Teilhard de Chardin.[83] Lee cites Teilhard to say that science and humanities are "not adversaries, but partners in the human quest."[84] Lee's nature and grace have merged into a single reality:

> . . . the issue is not whether God works intrinsically in man or in the teaching-learning dynamic, but how he works. In my own view, nature, teaching, learning, and man are not separated *in any*

---

[77] Lee, *Principles and Methods of Secondary Education* (New York: McGraw-Hill, 1963) 41, 61–62.

[78] Lee, *Shape*, 282 also 259; earlier, "Toward a Dialogue in Religious Instruction," 117.

[79] Lee, *Shape*, 284–86. Teilhard appears in Lee's writing as early as 1968's *Purpose of Catholic Schooling*, 41.

[80] Lee, "To Basically Change Fundamental Theory and Practice," 301–2.

[81] Lee, *Shape*, 289.

[82] Ibid., 272–81, 289, 292; *Flow*, 293, also 150, 177.

[83] The four are cited in Lee, *Shape*, 232, 272–81.

[84] In Lee's "Response to Dwayne E. Huebner," *Religious Education* 77 (1982) 394.

way over against God; rather nature is nature and can only be true because of the presence, power, and being of God in all nature. Wherever teaching and learning take place, God is intimately and existentially present *in every zone* of the process. Nature is not nature alone it is graced nature, or perhaps more precisely *grace-full nature*.[85]

The third support to the priority of God's immanence is a particular understanding of the way the Holy Spirit works. In brief, "[t]he Spirit works in and through life's conditions, not outside them or at odds with them."[86] Again, "God works through human and other natural agents in causing the behaviors he wishes."[87] Scarce reference to the Holy Spirit is found in Lee's writing, as at least one reviewer pointed out.[88] Taking in view four decades of writing, Lee places little emphasis on a possible need of educators to acknowledge unaccountable, directly supernatural, or miraculous aspects in teaching religion. One clear recognition occurs in *Shape*, where Lee writes, "To be sure, the work of the supernatural constitutes a central variable in the enterprise of religious instruction." There Lee seems to admit an unmeasurable, unpredictable, uncontrollable, supernatural intervention—and immediately lodges an objection: "the supernatural cannot be measured by empirical procedures . . . the evaluation and improvement of a particular religion class . . . [is] dependent upon the degree to which the learner's behavior is being modified along desired religious lines."[89] Lee's acknowledgment of transcendent supernatural action is rare. The infrequency is at least partly due to Lee's immanentist understanding of the work of the Spirit.[90]

Lee's employment of the theological term "revelation" is another reason why references to direct supernatural action are rare. Lee uses "revelation" to signify God's work in the learner. In other theological accounts, "conversion," or "sanctification," take some of the semantic field of his "revelation." For Lee, learning itself is revelation. Here he realized a parallel between progressive education's ways of knowing, and modern

---

[85] Lee, *Flow*, 292. The emphases are mine.
[86] Ibid., 177, 178, 179, 292, 293; *Purpose of Catholic Schooling*, 11.
[87] Lee, *Shape*, 100.
[88] Frederick K. Wilson observed five references in *Content*'s 784 pages. "The Content of Religious Instruction" [review], *Journal of Psychology and Theology* 13 (1985) 301–2.
[89] Lee, *Shape*, 188–89; *Flow*, 292; "Prediction in Religious Education," 48.
[90] "Authentic Source," 192–97.

theologies of revelation.[91] Revelation is ongoing in Vatican II influenced theologies. Lee's education theory resonates with the affirmation of the Council that revelation is not static truth; rather, revelation is in the developing cultural situation as well.[92] Accordingly, learning by experience is one way that God reveals himself in the world.

> The task of the religion class is to so structure and recast the learner's experience that God's ongoing revelation is consciously, meaningfully, and affectively incorporated into the person's self-system and behavioral patterns of action.[93]

Lee's understanding of faith goes with his desire for learning-as-revelation and performance outcomes. Faith becomes a construct built up of behaviors.[94] Since he defines religion as

> that form of *lifestyle* which *expresses and enfleshes* the lived relationship a person enjoys with a transpersonal being *as a consequence* of the actualized fusion in his self-system of that knowledge, belief, feeling, experience and practice that are in one way or another connected with that which the individual perceives to be divine . . . .[95]

so then,

> Faith is a construct. . . . To teach faith . . . is always to "teach about" . . . In order to teach faith as a personally lived reality and as a construct, the religious educator . . . teaches specifically for the attainment of one or more of these faith inclusive behaviors.[96]

---

[91] See *Shape*, 232–33 for instance.

[92] For example, Peter Hobson and Louise Welbourne, "Modal Shifts and Challenges for Religious Education in Catholic Schools Since Vatican II," *Christian Education Journal* 6 n.s. (Spring 2002) 56, drawing from the Council document on revelation, D. S. Amalorpavadass, and Kieran Scott.

[93] Lee, *Shape*, 16, also 15, 18, 27, 34, 36, 196, 230–33, 241; *Flow*, 295; "Toward a Dialogue in Religious Instruction," 117; "Prediction in Religious Education," 43–54.

[94] Lee, "Facilitating Growth in Faith," 270.

[95] Lee, "Authentic Source," 100. Also found in Lee, "Key Issues," 41. Cited in Mary C. Boys, "The Role of Theology in Religious Education," *Horizons* 11.1 (1984) 62; italics mine.

[96] Lee, "Facilitating Growth in Faith," 273–74; *Shape*, 211; *Flow*, 22. Possibly the insight derived from the parallel affirmation that learning is a construct. Performance, not learning, is observable. *Flow*, 45, 59.

Since Lee's definition of religion is functional, that is, what religion does in a person, his "faith" logically follows as "a human activity, a set of human behaviors."[97]

Lee sees confirmation of the social science approach in Jesus' own strategy. Jesus "operationalized" constantly.[98] Jesus modified Peter's behavior when he "taught" him faith. Jesus modified John's behavior by teaching him humility. The woman at the well (John 4:1-42) and the companions on the road to Emmaus (Luke 28:13-35) experienced Jesus as "modifying the behavior of all who would learn from him."[99] To Lee, each instance shows Jesus' focus on behavior. Further, Jesus met people in particular environments. "These environments were of a highly educative character because they represented situations which were intrinsically significant to the person or persons involved."[100] Thus Jesus used experience to teach, like a progressive educator. Lee is merely recovering the authentic method of Jesus. The selections from scripture highlight the method now known as the social science method of instruction.[101] The Bible, as Lee understands it, confirms his theory.

However, theology plays no positive role in Lee's education method. I mean by "method," the considered educative process, the theoretical account of the process, that which gives an account of the teaching-learning act. Theological material may well be included with the substantive contents, that is, the material that is taught. Is there theology in educational method? To use Lee's terms, is theology in the "structural" as well as the "substantive" or "material" contents? The answer is a definite "No." Lee says that theology must supply only "values" for the art-science of instruction. He writes, "The social-science approach to religious instruction is value-free in terms of any and all theologies. It can accommodate a Pelagian, an Augustinian, a Thomist, a Jansenist, or an advocate of the new theology."[102] A later list includes all kinds of faiths: Catholic, Mainline or Evangelical or Fundamentalist Protestant, "Jewish . . . Shinto . . . or whatever." Due to its value-free attribute, "[t]he religious instruction act, precisely because it is a social-science endeavor, can take on as many col-

---

[97] Lee, "Facilitating Growth in Faith," 270.
[98] Lee, *Shape*, 69, 191, 211; "Toward a Dialogue in Religious Instruction," 111; "Behavioral Objectives in Religious Education," 15; "Facilitating Growth in Faith," 270.
[99] Lee, *Shape*, 211.
[100] Lee, "Prediction in Religious Education," 46.
[101] Boys, *Biblical Interpretation*, 237.
[102] Lee, *Flow*, 292. Also Lee, "Religious Education and the Catholic University," 281.

orations as there are theologies . . . ."[103] One can accurately say of Lee's educational method that he means it to be theology-free.

Lee has little to say about theology's "valuing" work. He is relatively silent because social science religious instruction is the foundation for a variety of theologies, and the theory's application is for partisans of the various faiths. Because science is positive fact, theology is to supply interpretation only. Theology is to assign the meaning of the fact or ascribe the use to which fact is put. In no other aspect of his theory is interpretation more clearly separated from empirical observation than when Lee separates empirical fact from theology.

Indeed, to Lee the theory is valid precisely because of social science religious instruction's freedom from "values." Value-freedom is a must for Lee's conception of what theory is and does. "[N]o macrotheory which purports to explain, predict, verify, and enhance all religious phenomena can be theologically, politically, socially, or religiously particularistic."[104] Theory must be able to account for all the facts in its field. Theory must be neutral. Of course this conception of theory is well known, from the scientific method of René Descartes onward.

To Lee, independence from theology means his theory can increase co-operation. Where theology tends to divide religious educators from each other, social science religious instruction can allow for a plurality of religious commitments.[105] Because social science religious instruction is independent of theological commitments, educators across denominational and faith boundaries can use each other's work and learn from each other. Social science religious instruction thus fosters professional collaboration.[106]

Peer Reactions to Lee

Printed reaction to Lee is not easy to locate. Published interactions with the theory are far from numerous, in spite of the way that Lee was visible at professional conferences, was a full professor at a major university, a publisher, and prolific author.[107]

---

[103] Lee, *Content*, 42.

[104] Ibid., 42; "Religious Education and the Catholic University," *Notre Dame Journal of Education* 4 (1973) 276–83.

[105] Lee, "The Blessings of Religious Pluralism," in *Religious Pluralism and Religious Education* (Birmingham, Ala., Religious Education Press, 1988) 109–24.

[106] Lee, *Shape*, 4.

[107] Lee himself noticed the phenomenon, "Religious Instruction and Religious Experi-

Lee won support from a few colleagues in the field. Harold Burgess, whose dissertation under Lee became a widely used introductory text, gives enthusiastic approval. Burgess writes, "I believe that the social-science approach . . . may well prove to be the brightest hope for the future of religious education as a field and as a profession."[108] Burgess's main reason is that social science religious instruction is theology neutral and so able to draw together educationists of differing persuasions.[109] Another supporter is Robert O'Gorman, also a former doctoral student of Lee's. There are a small number of others.[110]

One location for traces of reaction to Lee is in religious education introductory texts. Mary Boys's survey, *Educating in Faith*, recognizes Lee among several post-catechetical theorists within Catholic religious education. She calls him an advocate for whole-person education, not merely cognitive or "head knowledge" education.[111] Jack Seymour's 1979 categorizing article places Lee as a proponent of empirical research for teacher professionalization. Seymour sees Lee as unrealistic, since "church school work [has] not seemed to transcend the situation of volunteer structures and teachers."[112]

Mary Boys's doctoral dissertation assesses Lee's contribution to the 1960s debate over the future of catechetics. Boys sees Lee's educational proposal as a factor, if a minor one, in its diminishing prominence. Salvation-historical catechetics was theology-based religious education. Its emergence was driven by particular hermeneutical presuppositions. It might have gained vital force from the affirmations of the Second Vatican Council, which drew from some of the same theological sources as had the catechetical model, but the heyday of salvation-historical catechetics proved a short one. According to Boys, the dominance of the Jungmann-Hofinger model of salvation-historical catechetics was eroded by theological, educational and cultural factors.[113] She identifies Lee's theory as an "outer space" proposal whose technological thrust helped to reduce confi-

---

ence," 543.

[108] Burgess, *An Invitation to Religious Education,* 168–69.
[109] Ibid., 169.
[110] Lee, "Social Science," 600.
[111] Boys, *Educating in Faith: Maps and Visions,* 157–58, 201.
[112] Jack L. Seymour, "Contemporary Approaches to Christian Education," 3–4.
[113] Mary C. Boys, *Educating in Faith,* 92–93; *Biblical Interpretation in Religious Education* analyses the fall of kerygmatic theology in religious education.

dence in salvation-historical catechetics.[114] Reaction in other dissertations is discussed below.

In an article, Boys assesses Lee's view of how educating relates to theology. Lee, according to Boys, sees theology and religious education as "distinct fields," rather than in other possible relationships, "subsumed" (theology as foundational) or "dialogical" (the disciplines gaining from each other). By comparison with peers, Lee grants theology the minimum of input.[115] Boys's assessment is echoed by others. Jeff Astley and others, introducing four alternative relationships of theology to education theory in an article collection, call Lee's "a very different voice." They note that Lee has "combatively distinguished his approach from any sort of theological approach."[116]

Another location for reaction to Lee is in reviews of his work. Reviews, while not exhaustive, nonetheless suggest critique. Howard Grimes, in a mainly positive 1974 review of *Flow*, writes that Lee "tends to be too uncritical of the social sciences, and does not recognize that social scientists have their own assumptions, some of which may get in the way of a valid approach to church education."[117] C. Ellis Nelson, also reviewing *Flow*, cautions against Lee's idea of the social sciences. "For almost any position taken by one social scientist, there can be found another social scientist who will take the opposite position." Nelson says that social sciences cannot be taken as value free, contrary to Lee, unless one excludes such obviously value-laden social scientists as Freud, Maslow, or Skinner.[118] Richard McBrien also points out Lee's attribution of value-freedom to social science.[119]

Lee replies to such criticism by attempting to clarify his conception of value-freedom in social science. He writes that social science is "not normative with respect to religious and moral values," that social science "cannot assign moral or religious value," and that social science can "deal with a wide variety of morally and religiously value-laden areas without having to . . . express a preference for one another (sic) value . . . ." Lee allows that "process contents," the structure or method of educating, might itself add

---

[114] Boys, *Biblical Interpretation*, 231–39.

[115] Boys, "The Role of Theology," 61–85.

[116] Astley, et. al., eds. *Theological Perspectives on Christian Formation*, 2.

[117] Howard Grimes, "Flow" [review], *Perkins Journal* 27 (1974) 59.

[118] C. Ellis Nelson, "The Flow of Religious Instruction," [review], *Living Light* 11.1 (1974) 146–48.

[119] Richard P. McBrien, "Toward an American Catechesis," *Living Light* 13.2 (1976) 175.

a "tint" to the theological color of the material contents. However, Lee never gives consideration to a possible tincture contributed by process. He denies any theological aspects to educational method.[120] Lee's conception of value-freedom is neutral social science adopting the values of a partner. Usage of social science is a sort of two-step with theology. In the actual practice of education, *someone's* social science always incorporates *someone's* theology, *someone's* confessional stance, *someone's* epistemology, as Ian Knox puts it.[121] "Values" are necessary and inevitable. In trying to clarify the value freedom of social science against his critics, Lee really affirms them by repeating that social science is able to support a variety of moral or religious "colorations."[122] Either Lee and his critics are talking past each other, or Lee is missing key perceptions of the critics. Precisely the issue is that Lee assigns valuing *in toto* to the theological partner. Lee's affirmation that social science adds little or no moral or religious coloration to the education process boils down to the admission of the value-free social science concept.

Some peers perceive Lee's understanding of theology to be unreasonably confined. Michael Warren writes that "Lee apparently fails to recognize that theology today does not see itself in terms of some disembodied "content of the revealed word of God." Theology is seen more as reflection on the religious experience of the Christian community."[123] Note, though, how Warren's clarification does not speak to Lee's whole concern. Lee's concern lies in his perception that theology is just cognition; Warren tags theology as "reflection," at least an act of cognition. Lee says that cognition is not the same thing as practice. "Religion is a way of life; theology is a theory about this way of life.[124] Cognition is inadequate to generate religious behaviors, because the whole person is not addressed.

Lee later specifies what he intends by "theology," providing a selection of theorists who place theology as speculative, cognitive, rational, or

---

[120] For example, Lee, "Authentic Source," 151, where Lee lambastes F. Darcy-Bérubé for a suggestion that theology has something to say about educational methods. Consistently Lee reads theology as importing particulars into a universal, and at this point he hears Darcy-Bérubé importing particular Roman Catholic theology into education. See below.

[121] Knox, *Above or Within?*, 92; Lee, *Content*, 36–37, 42.

[122] Lee, "Authentic Source," 132–33, n. 28; *Content*, 24, 42.

[123] Michael Warren, "All Contributions Cheerfully Accepted: Reflections on James Michael Lee," *Living Light* 7.4 (1970) 20–39.

[124] Lee, *Content*, 5, 7, 40; "Vision, Prophecy, and Forging the Future," 247, 256; "Authentic Source," 109.

even scientific in relation to its revealed data source.[125] The assessment that Lee has a narrow view of theology persists, however. Padraic O'Hare draws attention to the propositional character that Lee attributes to theology. O'Hare quotes Gabriel Moran to say that, contrary to Lee, theology is far from a closed system of established truths but is a "living dynamic search for the truth."[126] Richard McBrien writes that "Dr. Lee is seriously mistaken when he concludes that "theological science is primarily speculative rather than empirical; primarily deductive rather than inductive; primarily supernatural rather than natural; primarily rational rather than intuitive."[127] Mark Falbo's 1991 dissertation judges that Lee really rejected not theology but "a narrow, classical view of theology."[128]

Broadening the concern over Lee's treatment of theology, Françoise Darcy-Bérubé suggested at a late-1970s Boston College symposium that Lee indeed works from an underlying theology, an unacknowledged theology. Darcy-Bérubé, a Canadian Catholic pastoral theologian, proposes that the unaccounted theology "inspires and shapes both the behavioral outcomes the theory strives to facilitate and, indirectly, the pedagogical means or strategies it proposes."[129] Darcy-Bérubé insists that a teacher's theology will support or disallow certain teaching practices. Some teaching practices will be consistent with one's view of humanity, of God, of Church, and of Christian life; other practices will prove to be inconsistent. She points to brainwashing, indoctrination, pressure, or manipulation as unacceptable educational methods. Accordingly, theology must indeed be recognized as helping to struc-ture religious education as well as, of course, providing material content. Darcy-Bérubé urges that Lee recognize a legitimate, necessary role for theology in educational method and that he state his theology to promote professional dialogue.[130]

---

[125] *Shape*, 101–32; "Authentic Source," 108–9.

[126] Padraic O'Hare, "The Image of Theology in the Educational Theory of Lee," *Living Light* 11.3 (1974) 457. Lee took exception to O'Hare's essay, calling it "confused drivel," "Authentic Source," 171, n. 67.

[127] McBrien, "Toward an American Catechesis," *Living Light* 13.2 (1976) 175, cited in Coughlin, "Religious Education in Everyday Life," 142, n. 131.

[128] Mark Charles Falbo, "Theory and Praxis of Conversion in the Religious Education of Non-Poor Youth: An Educational Analysis of Bernard Lonergan on Conversion and Paulo Freire on Conscientization" (Ph.D. diss., Boston College, 1991) 197.

[129] Françoise Darcy-Bérubé, "The Challenge Ahead of Us," in *Foundations of Religious Education*, 118.

[130] Darcy-Bérubé, "The Challenge Ahead of Us," 118–19.

Darcy-Bérubé's piece drew searing footnotes in Lee's next major exposition, "The Authentic Source of Religious Instruction," published in 1982. He castigates her view that some teaching techniques are theologically unacceptable, saying that she really means "unacceptable from her partisan theological standpoint."[131] Darcy-Bérubé's view of theology, however, is not one of wooden propositions; for her, theology has enough finesse to be that which "inspires and shapes . . . the behavioral outcomes the theory strives to facilitate." The strength of Lee's reaction indicates a basic disagreement that will bear investigation.

Lee attributes resistance to his ideas to the "catechetical establishment."[132] He observes that major changes of methodology, such as his, require "a fundamental change in the personal self-organization and in the professional perception of . . . individuals in the field." Practitioners may resist such changes "vigorously and . . . irrationally."[133]

Educational Reactions

In terms of curriculum theory, Mary Boys observes that Lee's stress on measurable performance stands in the Tyler tradition of education.[134] Narrowly defined objectives are a hallmark of curriculum thinking that follows Ralph W. Tyler's *Basic Principles of Curriculum and Instruction*.[135] Tyler has a rational, goal-oriented approach to education. Tyler starts by recognizing the developmental stage of the learner, screens objectives through empirical findings of learning psychology, and tries to state objec-

---

[131] Lee, "Authentic Source," 121, n. 20; 149, n. 41; 151; 181, n. 79; 188, n. 86; 189, n. 88; 190, n. 91; 194, n. 97; 195, n. 98, n. 99. Lee's reaction is puzzling. He had written in *Flow* (1973) " . . . a teacher will teach a lesson quite differently if he views teaching as simply opening the pedagogical windows to let the Spirit blow where he wills (John 3:8) or, on the other hand, as purposeful behavior in which the teacher and other environmental variables exert predictable influences on the learner. A parent operating out of a Christian Science framework will suggest very different practices for a boy suffering from appendicitis than will a surgeon operating out of a natural science theory. An individual who views spiritual direction as a form of theological work will engage in far different kinds of practices than a person who considers spiritual direction as religious counseling and hence a mode of psychology." *Flow*, 42. The three alternated propositions that Lee implicitly recommends here are not recognized as theological. See below, Chapter 3.

[132] Lee, "To Basically Change Fundamental Theory and Practice," 310–12; Burgess, *An Invitation to Religious Education*, 129.

[133] Lee, *Content*, xiii.

[134] Boys, *Biblical Interpretation*, 233.

[135] Ralph W. Tyler, *Basic Principles of Curriculum and Instruction* (University of Chicago Press, 1949).

tives in a form to assist in selecting learning "experiences."[136] A reader of Lee immediately notices similar emphases and tone of scientific rigor. Lee cites Robert F. Mager's short book on instructional objectives in several places, saying that the book is "probably the best of its kind."[137] Mager also wants close specification of objectives in performance terms.

Some peers observe that Lee's educational method verges on behaviorism.[138] These critics are alerted by Lee's terminology—"behavioral modification,"[139] "manipulate," "variables,"[140] as well as his technical way of expressing himself.[141] The allegation of "behaviorism" is loaded, of course. "Behaviorism" evokes B. F. Skinner's operant conditioning psychology. The human subject is understood by the behaviorist to respond to stimuli like a machine.[142] Lee disavows any intention of manipulative behavior modification but he is willing to call his theory "behavioralism."[143] Lee complains that religious educators simply do not grasp social scientific vocabulary.[144] Lee's distinction between behaviorism and behavioralism maintains his intention: instructing is to be goal-directed for outward performances.

Lastly, combining educational and theological concerns, Kevin Coughlin sees that Lee may be advocating a human control of revelation. Since "revelation is accomplished through the teaching-learning process itself," and the religion class is to be structured to heighten revelation "both in itself and in the conscious awareness of the learner," Coughlin's suggestion seems a resonable inference.[145] Lee rejects this implication of his posi-

---

[136] Ibid., 5–15, 37–43.

[137] Lee, "Behavioral Objectives in Religious Education," 12–19; Robert F. Mager, *Preparing Instructional Objectives* (Palo Alto, Calif: Fearon, 1962) 13–43.

[138] Warren, "All Contributions Cheerfully Accepted," 29; Ruth L. Poochigian, "A Critical Analysis of Selected Roman Catholic Religious Education Theorists from the Perspective of Adult Education Research and Theory" (Ph.D. diss., University of Wisconsin—Madison, 1986) 113–16; O'Hare, "The Image of Theology," 454.

[139] Lee, *Flow*, 23, 46, 199.

[140] For example, Lee, "Authentic Source," 163 and "Toward a Dialogue in Religious Instruction," 118, just two samples of many.

[141] Lee, "Authentic Source," 135, is representative.

[142] Skinner's famous work was *Beyond Freedom and Dignity* (New York: Knopf, 1971). For Skinner, the right stimuli evoke the desired change. Skinner urged psychologists and counselees to move beyond the illusion of choice.

[143] Lee, *Flow*, 289–90.

[144] Lee, *Flow*, 278, affirmed by Darcy-Bérubé, "The Challenge Ahead of Us," 112.

[145] Coughlin, "Religious Education in Everyday Life," 196, quoting Lee, *Shape*, 237, 16.

tion, however.[146] As noted above, Lee occasionally allows for mysterious factors in the teaching-learning process, though never assigning weight to such uncontrollables. However, since Lee places so much stress on God's immanent presence in creation, and since instructional responsibility rests with the facilitator, Coughlin sees that Lee may be effectively saying that revelation can be facilitated predictably.

Summary

James Michael Lee's form of religious instruction is attuned to behavioral goals specified as closely as possible, to be governed by empirical findings like general education. Lee's stated theological basis is the identification of social science as God's immanent way of working in the world. Faith is an abstract construct that is really a cluster of characteristic behaviors. In this way, social science is identified nearly entirely with God's immanent working. In reaction, a small number of peers mostly disagreed.

The remainder of this study will show why social science religious instruction may not serve as a "macrotheory" for religious instruction, for two reasons. First, Lee urges one alternative of two for the significance of empirical research results, and second, because Lee, rather than setting forth a theology-neutral methodology, actually presents a methodology framed in a specific, but undeclared, theology. Chapter 2 will examine alternative ways to understand empirical findings.

---

[146] Lee writes against "theologically-oriented religious educationists" who argue against prediction of results. He said that any teacher predicts better results from a chosen method X than from method Y. Lee does not distinguish expectation from invariable prediction. *Flow*, 213, 348, n. 9.

2

Empiricism's Metaphysical Commitments

In a review of *The Flow of Religious Instruction,* the respected religious educator C. Ellis Nelson made a two-fold comment. He said that while Lee presents social science as a unified field, it is not. Lee presents social science as value-free "in terms of and in all specific theological positions." However, value-freedom "can be true only by restricting social science to . . . description or by excluding social scientists such as Sigmund Freud, Abraham Maslow, or B. F. Skinner—just to cite individuals from three schools of psychology who have taken positions that are not value-free."[1] Nelson's comment can be an opening from Lee's conception of the social sciences into a wider world. There is more than one methodological basis on which investigations may be conducted which are "social scientific."

The goal of this chapter is to show that empirical findings are not neutral, are not just "there." Instead, any empirical finding arises in a context that I will call "metaphysical." Metaphysics, or ontology, the nature of the cosmos, is one of three major divisions of philosophy, the others being epistemology and ethics. If metaphysical commitments happen also to be specifically theological commitments, empirical observation then could be said to happen in a theologically-committed context.

My procedure in this chapter is to trace the revolution in philosophy of science since 1950 by profiling three theorists. Then I relate insights to three theologians who seek to understand the social sciences theologically.

As Ellis Nelson said, the social sciences are plural. Mary Boys notes three main streams of sociology—*empirical, historical-philosophical-theological,* and *sociology of knowledge,* saying that each of these is "indis-

---

[1] C. Ellis Nelson, "The Flow of Religious Instruction" [review], *Living Light* 11 (1974) 146–48, quoting Lee, *Flow,* 292.

pensable to religious education."² Gregory Baum lists five types of sociology, including the classical sociological or social-scientific approach, positivistic-empirical sociology, functionalist sociology, critical sociology, and phenomenological sociology. *Classical sociologists* are Alexander Tocqueville, Karl Marx, Ferdinand Toennies, Emile Durkheim, Max Weber, Georg Simmel, and others. *Positivistic-empirical* sociology is that form "characterized by the attempt to assimilate sociology as much as possible to the natural sciences . . . concerned with the quantification and measurement of social action . . . to reach conclusions that are scientifically verifiable [where] the sociologist . . . thinks that the methods devised by him enable him to be in touch with the facts and draw valid conclusions independent of any theory." *Functionalist* sociologists bring a theoretical understanding of society as a system of social equilibrium into their research. The various functions of society serve the purpose of maintaining stability. *Critical theorists* see society as a system expressing ideologies which diminish humanity. Society alienates persons. *Phenomenological* sociology, lastly, wishes to "be in touch with the social process from within and clarifying through a systematic methodology what actually goes on in the creation of society."³ A third theorist, Robin Gill, distinguishes sociology in three streams: interactionist, functionalist, and Marxist. *Interactionist* is sociology like that of Max Weber, concerned with "the mutual interaction between ideas and behavior." *Functionalist* sociology is in the stream of the French theorist Emile Durkheim where social phenomena are analyzed in terms of the role they perform. Society in functionalist sociology is conceived as in equilibrium; functions contribute to an existing balance. *Marxist* sociology follows Marx in seeing society as constructed by ideology.⁴

The point of listing these typologies is to show that one social science, sociology, is far from unitary. Diversity is found in other social disciplines too. In psychology Edmund Sullivan, proposing a critical methodology, says that it is a "misnomer" to call the discipline "internally coherent." While topics such as clinical psychology, personality psychology or learning psychology appear side by side in introductory texts, to Sullivan "the closest relationship between these areas of concern is their proximity to

---

² Boys, *Educating in Faith*, 171.
³ Gregory Baum, "Sociology and Theology," *Concilium* 1.10 (1974) 22–31.
⁴ Robin Gill, "Introduction," in *Theology and Sociology: A Reader*, enl. ed., ed. Robin Gill (London: Cassell, 1996) 2.

each other (spatially, not conceptually) in the text."[5] The commonality among the disciplines is their desire to be scientific, not to "armchair it" as would a philosopher.[6] The typologies show that social science is not empiricism only but includes a variety of approaches.

Lee's "social science" is the "empirical" type of Baum and Boys. Lee says that he intends by the term "social science," "anthropology, economics, education, geography, history, law, political science, psychiatry, psychology, and sociology,"[7] saying that "social science" is a generic term for human study disciplines.[8] Social science for Lee is that "confluence of disciplines that . . . explains, predicts and verifies human behavior.[9] The verbs, "explain," "predict," and "verify," are important to Lee, and recur in his writing.[10] By "explain," "predict," and "verify," Lee is describing a particular method found in "economics, anthropology" and other social science disciplines. As detailed in chapter 2, Lee's social science is replicable; its findings will be obtained again when a study is repeated.[11] The personality of the researcher will not get in the way because he or she has procedures that enable him to be a neutral observer.[12] A fact is an observed and tested phenomenon;[13] and a theory is an edifice built of solid facts.[14] Social science is value free;[15] facts simply "are."[16]

---

[5] Edmund V. Sullivan, *A Critical Psychology: Interpretation of the Personal World* (New York: Plenum, 1984) viii.

[6] Christopher G. A. Bryant, *Positivism in Social Theory and Research* (Basingstoke, Eng.: Macmillan, 1985) 144.

[7] "Authentic Source," 130.

[8] Lee, *Shape*, 134.

[9] "Authentic Source," 130.

[10] For example, Lee, *Content*, xiv, 42; *Toward a New Era*, 120; "Religious Instruction and Religious Experience," 541; "Authentic Source," 120, 132–35; also "The Social-Science Approach To Religious Instruction," [videorecording] (Birmingham, Ala: Religious Education Press, 1999).

[11] Lee, *Shape*, 136.

[12] Ibid., 138; *Content*, x; "Social science," 599.

[13] Lee, *Shape*, 154.

[14] Ibid., 156, 158; "Toward a New Era: A Blueprint for Positive Action," in *The Religious Education We Need: Toward The Renewal Of Christian Education*, ed. James Michael Lee (Mishawaka, Ind: Religious Education Press, 1977) 120; "To Basically Change Fundamental Theory and Practice," in *Modern Masters of Religious Education*, ed. Marlene Mayr (Birmingham, Ala: Religious Education Press, 1983) 299.

[15] Lee, *Shape*, 207.

[16] Lee, "Authentic Source," 117, 132–33.

Lee is not the first empiricist, of course. He is within a tradition that stretches to the beginning of the modern era, with traces in the earliest Greek thinking.[17] The *Cambridge Dictionary of Philosophy* defines empiricism as "a type of theory in epistemology, the basic idea behind all examples of the type being that experience has primacy in human knowledge and justified belief."[18] Empiricism is an assertion about what can be taken as solid knowledge. Empiricism is an affirmation about verification. It prescribes conditions for taking observations as reliable or "true." In education, G. Stanley Hall was an empiricist whose Child Study Movement placed new emphasis on the developmental readiness of the child.[19] John Dewey, influential twentieth century philosopher of education, is an empiricist, albeit a modified one.[20] In Dewey's view, experience in its form of "objective observation and experimentation implies direct, first-hand, fresh contact with the phenomena of nature, society and man," in contrast to the "stale repetition and blind acceptance of conventional and traditional 'truth.'"[21] Dewey's observer, as usual for empiricists, is invisible. The observer is neutral. His or her "direct, first-hand contact" seems to add nothing to data.

Empirical observation continues to wield significant authority in modern culture, but current philosophies of science have placed numerical measures in a larger perspective. In North America the perspective was opened by Thomas S. Kuhn's philosophy of science, built on work by W. V. Quine, N. R. Hanson, and others. Kuhn's insights have become so mainstream in North American academic culture that an exhaustive account is unnecessary. I provide a synopsis of Kuhn and others to commence a critique of empiricism. Then I proceed to current philosophy of the social sciences, mainly by way of sociology.

---

[17] Gordon Clark, *From Thales to Dewey* (Jefferson, Md: Trinity Foundation, 1985) 5–8; *Cambridge Dictionary of Philosophy*, 2d ed., s.v. "Thales of Miletus," gen. ed. Robert Audi (Cambridge: Cambridge University Press, 1999).

[18] *Cambridge Dictionary of Philosophy*, 2d ed., s.v. "Empiricism."

[19] Joop W. A. Berding, *John Dewey's Participatory Philosophy of Education: Education, Experience and Curriculum* (Leiden: DWSO, 1999).

[20] Dewey's conception of truth is pragmatic. His criterion for truth is that which is useful to the advancement of the human race; truth is what is useful for us to believe. Objective truth is unknowable. Dewey is half a "logical empiricist."

[21] Johannes Van der Ven, *Practical Theology: An Empirical Approach* (Kampen: Kok Pharos, 1993) 6, quoting Dewey.

A New Paradigm in Philosophy of Science

Kuhn's major work was *The Structure of Scientific Revolutions*.[22] Kuhn sought to reconstruct the process of major scientific change, using new historical accounts. He analyzed the process of "discovery" that allows what is obviously true to the eyes of generations of observers become yesterday's truth for a succeeding generation. In his telling, the new astronomical theory of Copernicus overturned Ptolemaic astronomy not by superior observations, not by factoring new data into the Ptolemaic universe model, but by entirely supplanting Ptolemy's paradigm with a rival system of explanation. As seen by Kuhn, the paradigm is a disciplinary matrix or an exemplar, a template, which makes sense of observations.[23] The earlier system of scientific explanation acknowledges inexplicable phenomena but to eliminate conflict treats them as modifications of the theory. In the old paradigm unexplainable data is included as anomalies. Satisfactory explanation only comes when a paradigm arises which includes the previously unexplainable via a scientific "revolution." In 1962 accretion was the standard conception of scientific change. By accretion, science more and more closely approximates reality. Kuhn saw that science does not proceed by a steadily growing body of data; instead, paradigm supplants paradigm in the way that Einstein's physics of relativity supplanted the older Newtonian physics.

In a striking reversal, Kuhn saw that data itself depends on theory. Observations are not merely accounted for but are *made* with theory. Only when pressure is brought to bear will a new paradigm arise that accounts for anomalies. Galileo was able to bring such pressure with a new instrument, the telescope—only to have his critics refuse to look into it! The critics felt no need to see for themselves. Why should they look? Their existing paradigm satisfied them. Facts are not independent of theory; what one wants or expects to see is what, most times, one does see.[24] Indeed, it appears that new paradigms are accepted through attrition as the former generation retires and a new generation arises which takes up the replace-

---

[22] Kuhn, *The Structure of Scientific Revolutions*, 2d ed. (Chicago: University of Chicago Press, 1970).

[23] Kuhn was accused of an ambiguous notion of "paradigm" after the first edition (1962) and clarified the term in a postscript to the 1970 second edition.

[24] Lee could be especially aware that a new theory generates resistance. He states that his own system met resistance because it challenges existing institutional arrangements. He names the arrangements the "Central Catechetical Establishment." Lee, "To Basically Change Theory and Practice," 310–12.

ment paradigm. The new paradigm is not absorbed into the older paradigm but supplants it. A new way of seeing eclipses older facts.

By contrast, Lee presents his theory as built on solid facts, facts established by the three-fold scientific method of explanation, prediction, and verification. For Lee, facts are not entwined with theory. "Facts simply are: they have no meaning and significance in and of themselves."[25] Lee's facts are raw or brute facts. The interconnectedness of facts and theory, on the other hand, is what Kuhn showed North Americans. A fact is a fact only within a system of reference. What were facts for Ptolemy are facts no more. Newtonian facts, set in a theory that explained the physical world well up to a point, were superseded in the twentieth century by new facts. The new facts are based on a series of insights that resulted in a new paradigm, one incorporating quantum mechanics.

Quantum mechanics is especially interesting for the understanding of "fact" because Werner Heisenberg and others, discovering the apparent paradox that light is emitted not only in waves but in packets (quanta), discovered also that the observer and the observed are not separate. The phenomenon moves under the very act of observation—one thinks of Heisenberg's uncertainty principle, or the falling pitch of a train whistle as the train moves from the listener.

Observer and the observed interact. The fact changes under observation. This kind of conceptualization is far different from Lee's building-block theory of fact, and challenges it. The interactivity of subject and object takes a different form in the social sciences as we will see, but the involvement of observer with object is especially significant there.

Kuhn's theory had precursors in North America and Europe, many cited in *Structure of Scientific Revolutions*. W. V. Quine, Harvard philosopher, published against "Two Dogmas of Empiricism," in 1951. Quine broke down a ground rule of the school of Logical Positivism, and showed that the boundary between natural science and metaphysics is not so rigid as was thought. "Modern empiricism," said Quine, "has been conditioned . . . by two dogmas. One is a belief in some fundamental cleavage between truths which are . . . grounded in meanings independent of matters of fact, and truths which are grounded in fact. . . ."[26] Quine showed on purely

---

[25] Lee, "Authentic Source," 117; 120; "Toward a New Era," 120; "To Basically Change Theory and Practice," 299. An earlier statement (*Shape*, 158) seems to recognize interrelationships among fact, law, and theory but the later statements are more characteristic. Compare for instance, *Flow*, 39: "Theory . . . explains how and why seemingly disparate and unconnected facts are related or integrated; . . ."

[26] Quine, "Two Dogmas of Empiricism," in *The Theory of Knowledge: Classical and Con-*

logical grounds that any attempt to mark off "analytic" from "synthetic" statements was not likely to produce clarity. The second dogma is reductionism, "the belief that each *meaningful* statement is equivalent to some logical construct upon terms which refer to *immediate experience.*"[27] Quine denied that only experience gives justified true belief. Against the Logical Positivists, non-empirical statements are not literally meaningless. Quine said significantly that "[o]nly as a *corporate body* do the statements of a theory face the tribunal of experience."[28] "Two Dogmas" was a building block for Kuhn.

Another Kuhn forerunner was N. R. Hanson. Hanson's 1958 book *Patterns of Discovery* included a chapter entitled "Observation." Hanson showed that though philosophers and others separated observation from interpretation, observation is already interpretive, that is, already theory-laden. We casually say we saw the sun rise, as if it were an observation identical to all observers. But the astronomer Johannes Kepler and his contemporary Tyco Brahe did not see the same thing when they watched the sun. Brahe viewed a sun moving in an earth-centered universe. Kepler saw the "same" sun as fixed. Interpretation is embedded in observation. Another of Hanson's instances is well known. Shown a drawing that may be interpreted in two ways, one viewer perceives the face of the Parisian old woman, while another viewer can only see a young woman dressed in flowing clothes à la Toulouse-Lautrec. Each viewer sees what they see without any later act of interpretation.[29] Hanson's account of the factors involved in seeing a "new" sun foreshadowed Kuhn's elaboration of paradigm change.

A third precursor of Kuhn was Michael Polanyi, cited by Kuhn like the previous two. Polanyi showed in *Personal Knowledge* (1958) that philosophical presuppositions underlie all scientific research.[30] He placed presuppositions in a tacit, not recognized dimension of knowledge. The tacit dimension may include assumptions from the religious and cultural heritage of the scientist. The presence of the tacit dimension means that a par-

---

temporary Readings, ed. Louis P. Pojman (Belmont, Calif: Wadsworth, 1993) 395, emphasis mine.

[27] Quine, "Two Dogmas of Empiricism," 395.

[28] *Cambridge Dictionary of Philosophy*, 2d ed., s.v. "Quine, Willard Van Orman," also Quine, "Two Dogmas," 395–407.

[29] Norwood Russell Hanson, "Observation," in *Science, Reason, and Reality: Issues in the Philosophy of Science*, ed. Daniel Rothbart (Fort Worth: Harcourt Brace, 1998) 77–95.

[30] Michael Polanyi, *Personal Knowledge: Toward a Post-Critical Philosophy* (Chicago: University of Chicago Press, 1958).

adigm may be functioning even if a full set of rules cannot be articulated. For instance, some elements of the paradigm may be commonly known by persons of the scientific community from experience in the field.

Besides these three theorists, there is a body of European philosophy of science cited by Kuhn. Among those cited is Ludwik Fleck, a Polish Jewish scholar who anticipated by decades much of what has been sustained of Kuhn's thesis.[31]

Kuhn, then, led a paradigm change of his own within philosophy of science. His insight that facts and theory, observation and interpretation, subject and object, are not entirely separable will be echoed in theorists examining methodology in the social sciences.

Lee Not a Positivist?

A philosophy of science that separates fact from interpretation is technically termed a "positivism." There are few positivists now to be found.[32] It is unlikely that a social scientist would own up to the label.

The absence of confessing positivists is due in North America to the Kuhnian revolution. Kuhn's concerns have had more impact in the social sciences than in physical science.[33] Kuhn made his case by a historical account rather than by analysis, the kind of pure theory preferred by hard scientists. Further, his work seemed to imply relativism. He seemed to say that a superseded system of understanding was no less true to reality than systems that followed it. He seemed to deny that human beings can know what is real. Scientific revolutions were based as much on the power of a dominant group of scientists as on merit of argument: paradigm shifts seemed to be irrational. Accordingly, physical scientists, from whose research come technological wonders, seem to be unaffected by Kuhn's work. Physical scientists proceed with tacitly realist science in positive

---

[31] This insight comes from a discussion among religious studies scholars through the world wide web listserv group "Nu-Rel," especially a March 31, 1998 posting addressed to me by Brigitte Schoen of the University of Bonn.

[32] Leszek Kolakowski, *Positivist Philosophy: From Hume to the Vienna Circle* (Harmondsworth, Eng.: Penguin, [1966] 1972) 9–19; David Frisby, "Introduction to the English Translation," in *The Positivist Dispute in German Sociology*, Theodor W. Adorno et al., trans. Glyn Adey and David Frisby (London: Heinemann [1969] 1976) ix; Bryant, *Positivism in Social Theory*, 1.

[33] Edward Rothstein, "Coming to Blows Over How Valid Science Really Is," *New York Times* (July 21, 2001) B9.

fashion, apparently untroubled by the inner connection between fact and value—to the chagrin of some.[34]

Not so the social scientists. Kuhn's first consideration of scientific change appears to have arisen as he observed, not physical scientists, but social scientists. As a young professor Kuhn witnessed disagreements among social scientists on "the nature of legitimate scientific problems and methods. . . . Controversies over fundamentals . . . seem(ed) endemic among say, psychologists or sociologists."[35] Basing his case for paradigms of theory and fact on hard science, Kuhn established a "strong" thesis readily accepted by some seeking appropriate methods for human sciences. Social sciences, now as then, appear to be fields without a reigning paradigm. Social sciences are still fields in which "investigators are casting about for a fundamental insight that will bring order into a disparate field."[36] Typologies of three, or five, sociologies does not exhaust possible paradigms, since each sociology includes numbers of schools of thought. Kuhn brought clarity merely by saying that the social sciences are in search of a dominant paradigm, are "preparadigmatic." Competing paradigms of theory and fact are visible in any of the social sciences.

Lee naturally denies that he is a positivist. Writing against the charge, Lee narrowly defines positivism only as a set of stipulations that

> [m]etaphysics does not exist; God either does not exist or he is unknowable; theology is nothing more than superstition; all claims about knowledge of transcendence must be rejected . . . I affirm the validity of metaphysics in areas in which it is competent. I affirm the existence and knowability of God . . . I affirm the validity of knowledge of transcendent beings and forces.[37]

Metaphysics, as Lee intimates, is indeed a "theoretical philosophy of being and knowing."[38] More exactly, it is the "philosophical investigation of the nature, constitution, and structure of reality."[39] Lee continues, "I do ac-

---

[34] Sandra Harding, *The Science Question in Feminism* (Ithaca: Cornell University Press, 1986) 34, also comments in D. C. Phillips and Nicholas Burbules, *Postpositivism and Educational Research* (Lanham, Md.: Rowman and Littlefield, 2000) 60–61.

[35] Kuhn, *Scientific Revolutions,* viii.

[36] Vern S. Poythress, *Science and Hermeneutics,* Foundations of Contemporary Interpretation 6 (Grand Rapids: Zondervan, 1988) 46.

[37] Lee, "Key Issues in the Development of a Workable Foundation for Religious Instruction," in *Foundations of Religious Education,* ed. Padraic O'Hare (New York: Paulist, 1978) 59–60.

[38] *Oxford Concise Dictionary of Current English,* 5th ed., s.v. "metaphysics."

[39] *Cambridge Dictionary of Philosophy,* 2d ed., s.v. "metaphysics."

cept certain principles of positivism such as the emphasis on experience," but "to accept certain principles is in no way tantamount to accepting the entire philosophy. . . . The social science approach is value-free, so it can be used by a positivist or by an antipositivist."[40]

I quote extensively because the statement discloses the issues. I will examine several elements. Lee is not against metaphysics. But, outright denial of metaphysics is not the only way to be a positivist. Positivism takes more than one form. One might effectively bypass, or minimize, metaphysics. I will show that Lee is a positivist but not the usual kind.

Lee is correct that outright denial of metaphysics is an attribute of positivism in its classic sociological form. The first "positive philosophy" was that of Auguste Comte (1798–1857), a French crusader who is also accorded the usual credit for founding sociology. Comte denied human ability to know ultimate causes or the nature of things-in-themselves. Comte had a phenomenalist attitude to the world, and to him, the human task is to "boil down the multiplicity of phenomena to laws."[41] Metaphysics contributed only ungrounded speculation about matter.[42] Comte posited three eras of human development, the mythical, the theological, and the positive. A "fact in Comte's theory is shorn of its psychic [metaphysical] background, it is a reality *sui generis*."[43] The major school of twentieth-century positivism, the Logical Positivism of Rudolf Carnap or A. J. Ayer, also denied metaphysics.[44]

Lee does not deny metaphysics in simple fashion. He writes, for instance, "the issue is not whether God works intrinsically in man or in the teaching-learning dynamic, but how he works,"[45] and the citations could be multiplied twenty-fold. Just a few will shed light on how Lee sees the issue. In *Principles and Methods of Secondary Education* (1963) he claimed, "The temporal and eternal, natural and supernatural, should never be

---

[40] Lee, "Key Issues," 60.

[41] Kolakowski, *Positivist Philosophy*, 85.

[42] *Cambridge Dictionary of Philosophy*, 2d ed., s.v. "Comte, Auguste."

[43] Kolakowski, *Positivist Philosophy*, 84; also Christopher G. A. Bryant, *Positivism in Social Theory and Research* (Basingstoke, Eng.: Macmillan, 1985) 111.

[44] Bryant, *Positivism in Social Theory*, 2; Douglas Sloan, *Faith and Knowledge* (Louisville: Westminster John Knox, 1994) 123. Advocacy for Logical Positivism originated in a 1928 manifesto published by Austrian academics calling themselves the "Vienna Circle." Philosophical circles in Britain and America were more or less close to Vienna positivism; A. J. Ayer and Sir Karl Popper were not members of the literal Vienna Circle but advocated similar positions.

[45] Lee, *Flow*, 292.

separated in Catholic secondary education."[46] In 1990, Lee wrote, "while God's grace is totally responsible in the ultimate analysis for a person's coming to faith, it is God's grace flowing through the human activity of religious instruction which proximately and effectually gives rise to the acquisition of faith."[47]

However, a positivist may deny metaphysics in more than one way. Christopher Bryant agrees with Lee that positivism has been associated

> with *epistemologies* which make experience the foundation of all knowledge, and also with their complementary *ontologies* which propose a division between objects which are accessible to observation (about which knowledge is therefore possible) and objects which are not (and about which there can therefore be no knowledge).[48]

As a guide to help identify a positivism, Bryant provides identification marks from the Polish philosopher Leszek Kolakowski, and also from Anthony Giddens. Bryant recapitulates Kolakowski's identifiers: "Positivism asserts the claims of experience as the ultimate foundation of human knowledge and denies the possibility of meaningful discourse concerning supersensible objects."[49] Let us take the clauses separately.

Firstly, knowledge worthy of the name must come by experience only. An assertion is held to be literally meaningless unless it can be verified.[50] The "verifiability criterion of meaning" is the driving tenet of Logical Positivism. That driving tenet is similar in other positivisms.

Lee definitely resonates to verification by experience. He does not claim experience for the ultimate foundation of human knowledge, but he claims it for "proximate" knowledge. Proximate knowledge is the kind that counts in the here-and-now: "Social science is characterized by close adherence to observable data so that whatever conclusion is reached from the

---

[46] Lee, *Principles and Methods*, 61.

[47] Lee, "Introduction," in *Handbook of Faith*, ed. James Michael Lee (Birmingham, Ala.: Religious Education Press, 1990) 271.

[48] Bryant, *Positivism in Social Theory*, 1.

[49] Ibid., 3, quoting Barry Hindess, *Philosophy and Methodology in the Social Sciences* (Hassocks, Eng.: Harvester, 1977) 16. Echoed by, for example, *Cambridge Dictionary of Philosophy*, s.v. "Positivism"; *Encyclopedia Britannica*, s.v. "Epistemology," retrieved from <http://www.brittanica.com> on July 14, 2000.

[50] *Cambridge Dictionary of Philosophy*, s.v. "Logical Positivism." Also Sloan, *Faith and Knowledge*, 123; Bryant, *Positivism in Social Theory*, 114.

investigation follows naturally from the observable procedure rather than from sources which are speculatively authoritative, or uncontrolled."[51]

The education that Lee wishes to measure empirically is God at work without apparent complication: "Most proponents of the theological approach to religious instruction needlessly befog religious instruction endeavor by claiming that the Holy Spirit is not only the ultimate cause of religious instruction activity but the single proximate cause as well."[52]

Equally, on the metaphysical side: "There can be no ultimate conflict between theology and the nontheological sciences because in the final analysis there are no nontheological propositions or data which assert anything fundamentally meaningful about foundational realities such as God, grace, revelation, and religion."[53]

Lee makes an entire separation between religious or ultimate reality, and this-world reality. To Lee, theological reflection on the nature of the teaching-learning process has no place. Lee affirms metaphysics, yes, but it is metaphysics that has nothing to do with this-world action. For those with eyes to see, enough truth for this world is right there. Empirical measurement tells the tale.

> [T]he broad framework and thrust of the instructional process qua social science are such that they are sufficiently congruent to theological science. As a consequence, theology can be quite at ease and natural in its harmonious working relationship with social science. The points of contact between the two are many and *complementary*.[54]

To repeat the Kolakowski identifer, positivisms deny "the possibility of meaningful discourse concerning supersensible objects." The key word is "meaningful." Lee sees no conflict between empirical social science and theology. They are compatible because social science is measuring not the ultimate world (that would be impossible) but rather the proximate world. "[R]eligion is a human phenomenon and therefore is amenable to empirical as well as to nonempirical investigation."[55] Lee is somewhat like Kant who envisaged two worlds, a phenomenal world that can be investigated and known, and a noumenal world which is beyond sense experience.

---

[51] Lee, *Shape*, 136.
[52] Lee, "Authentic Source," 193.
[53] Ibid., 148.
[54] Lee, *Shape*, 227, emphasis mine.
[55] Lee, Flow, 295.

In the visible world, Lee's God works in such a way that secular means are the same as religious means. God does not work one way in general education and another way in religious education. God is at work in the world, period. Lee never registers that the world is not according to original design. He does not note that the world is askew. The presence of evil and the general dislocation of human living are not factored into his theory. Lee's God is immanent. God can be discovered in the secular world in straight-forward fashion.

Lee fits easily into Baum's positivistic-empirical sociology category. Lee clearly is concerned with the quantification and measurement of social action and "tries to reach conclusions that are scientifically verifiable." Lee definitely believes that, in Baum's typology, "the methods devised by him enable him to be in touch with the facts and draw valid conclusions independent of any theory." For Lee, social science and theology relate as "data" relates to "values." Social science provides the data for which theology prescribes the use. In this division of labor, it is sociology's work to describe the world as it is; theology's share of labor is to relate a neutral sociological description to the world as it ought to be. To Lee, empirical studies describe reality as found by neutral scientists with their variety of conceptual measuring tools. Theology will then prescribe what should be done to modify present reality. Lee is thus able to write that social science can accommodate any theological view whatsoever.[56] Lee is not against metaphysics, as long as contained in an other-worldly compartment. By the same token, Lee's data is uncontaminated by metaphysics. Therefore, Lee's understanding of data is positivistic.

An Alternative Social Science

After Kuhn, a "hermeneutical turn" was marked in the social sciences, by some at least. Interest in social science methodology reached theology. For example, a session of the 2001 Canadian Theological Society meeting examined the methodology of research on a student group's function for evangelicals in a university.[57] Theologians take philosophy of social science to clarify how social sciences are used for theological research.

---

[56] Lee, *Content*, 42.

[57] David Seljak, "Some Critical Questions for Paul Bramadat's *The Church on the World's Turf* (May 24, 2001, Laval University, Ste-Foy, Quebec). Retrieved from <http://www3.sympatico.ca/ian.ritchie/SeljakonBramadat.html> on Nov. 11, 2001; John Stackhouse Jr., "An Anthropologist Bonds with a Tribe called 'InterVarsity Christian Fellowship,'" *Books & Culture* 7.6 (2001) 22.

In this section I profile insights of Gregory Baum, Don Browning, and John Milbank in relation to Lee's theory. Identifying what "social science" means after Kuhn will highlight what Lee's theory overlooks.

Gregory Baum

Gregory Baum is a German-Canadian theologian who seeks to bring sociological insight to theology. Baum traced theology's relation to sociology, specifically. Baum came to theology after training in mathematics. He confesses that his late-1960s interest in sociology was driven by frustration. A Catholic, he

> could not understand why the Catholic Church, despite the good will of clergy and laity and the extraordinary institutional event of Vatican II, had been unable to move and adopt the new style of Catholicism outlined in the conciliar documents. I thought that sociology, as the systematic inquiry into society, should be able to answer this question.[58]

Note that the apparent inadequacy of theology to explain a social circumstance was the factor to spur Baum's study; similarly, the inadequacy of dogma for teaching methods prompted Lee's social science turn. One naturally expects that Baum will present himself as a mediator and advocate for a sociological way of seeing. He does come as a mediator—but not of sociology's empirical form.

In *Religion and Alienation* (1975), Baum resolved the five types listed at the start of the chapter into just two, an objective sociology, "Sociology O," and hermeneutical sociology, "Sociology H." Baum opts for Type "H." Sociology H, like Sociology O, still asks that researchers attempt to abandon bias and undertake replicable research. But Sociology H insists that value-neutral sociology is an illusion. Researchers must "clarify their historical relationship to the object they study" and "become conscious of the ideal of society they carry in their minds."[59] Otherwise, their conclusions will be unwittingly distorted. Baum's reduction to two basic types is paralleled by Gerard Radnitzky, a Polish philosopher of science, whose major work discerned a technical or toolmaking type like "O" and a "question raising" type like "H."[60]

---

[58] Gregory Baum, *Religion and Alienation: A Theological Reading of Sociology* (New York: Paulist, 1975) 1.

[59] Baum, *Religion and Alienation*, 258.

[60] Gerard Radnitzky, *Contemporary Schools of Metascience*, 2d rev. ed., Vol. 1: *Anglo-Saxon Schools of Metascience* (Göteborg: Scandinavian University Books, 1970) 15.

Baum notes that theologians as far back as Ernst Troeltsch have raised doubts about the possibility of sociologists observing in any neutral or value-free way. Troeltsch's *Social Teaching of the Christian Churches* (1911) "demonstrated that sociologists, whether they realize it or not, bring with them their own world as they do their research. They can arrive at a reliable reading of their object of study only if they are willing to explore how their own conceptual world relates to the world of their object of study." Troeltsch observed that a "colonizer cannot credibly study the colonized without a change in personal consciousness."[61] This insight is paralleled by Peter Winch, the analytic Oxford philosopher, who wrote a philosophy of social science in 1959. Winch said that "A monk has certain characteristic social relations with his fellow monks and with people outside the monastery" but one could hardly "give more than a superficial account of those relations without taking into account the religious ideas around which the monk's life revolves."[62]

Moreover, Troeltsch saw that "observers, even if they tried, could not separate the 'is' from their perception of the 'ought.'"[63] Troeltsch's insight implies that what the observer perceives depends, at least in part, on what he or she expects to see. The observer is not separated from the act of observation. The person cannot be abstracted from the act of observing. His or her values already are present in what is seen.

In a brief 2000 survey presentation, Baum specifies four ways that the researcher's values shape the research project.

> 1. The questions asked are drawn from ideals. The values of the researcher or the institution are reflected in the very questions posed.

---

[61] Baum, "Remarks of a Theologian," 4; also Miroslav Volf, "Soft Difference: Theological Reflections on the Relation Between Church and Culture in 1 Peter," *Ex Auditu* 10 (1994) 15–16. Volf reminds readers that H. R. Niebuhr admitted that his five-fold typology in *Christ and Culture* could be said to depend on Troeltsch's typology of church and sect. That Mary Boys draws from Niebuhr is evident from the first pages of *Educating in Faith*. The reader may detect a genealogy of the present study's paradigm analysis.

[62] Peter Winch, *The Idea of a Social Science* (London: Routledge & Kegan Paul, 1990) 23. To affirm the need to be careful about those with alternate worldviews will not necessarily mean solipsism. D. C. Phillips and Nicholas Burbules affirm the study of others' reality; one does not have to be e.g. white Anglo-Saxon Protestant to research them. *Postpositivism*, 48–50.

[63] Baum, "Remarks of a Theologian in Dialogue with Sociology," in *Theology and the Social Sciences*, ed. Michael Horace Barnes (Maryknoll, N.Y.: Orbis, 2001) 4.

2. Research is driven by an intention, a personal motivation. Research is labor-intensive, time-consuming, demanding. The question must be personally compelling, that is to say, value-driven, if the project is to be sustained.

3. A model is used to organize data. The chosen model inevitably guides and hides or masks aspects of the object(s).

4. The researcher, being human, is related in some way to the object(s) of study. The researcher may be relatively detached from or drawn toward the object of study.[64]

Values thus enter into research in multiple ways. The way values affect research is seen in conflicting conclusions. For instance, Baum notes that the question of whether globalization is death-dealing or life-promoting has not been resolved by research. The reason for conflicting results is the subjectivity that each scientist brings to his or her study. Their values differ. The identical scientific method will produce different results from differing observers.[65]

Baum says that "[Sociology O] does not sufficiently recognize the influence of personal presuppositions on sociological research and the impossibility of presup-positionless science."[66] The observer is himself or herself a part of that which he or she is observing. He or she is involved socially and politically, that is, personally involved. Necessarily a moral stance is taken with respect to the object of social study: an ideal, "a vision of what might be determines what the sociologist says is."[67] It is as impossible to separate one's ideals from one's observations as to detach seeing from the mind.

---

[64] Baum, "Remarks," 8. Baum's comments are paralleled by Elliot Eisner in *The Educational Imagination* (New York: Macmillan, 1979) 46: "Descriptive theory is in a subtle but important sense pervaded by normative theory because the methods of inquiry we chose and the criteria we chose to apply to test truth claims reflect beliefs about the nature of knowledge..."

[65] Baum, "Remarks," 9.

[66] Baum, *Religion and Alienation*, 259–60.

[67] Baum, *Religion and Alienation*, 137; the quote is by Roderick Martin in "Sociology and Theology: Alienation and Original Sin," in *Theology and Sociology: A Reader*, ed. Robin Gill (London: Cassell, 1996) 113; see also Browning, *Religious Thought*, 15ff.

Baum says that the basic mistake is supposing subject and object to be wholly distinct:

> In the English-speaking world, philosophers and educated people in general . . . have regarded as outrageous and contrary to common sense the . . . claim that the structure of the human mind enters into the production of the historical and cosmic reality. People tend to take for granted that the world is a . . . finished object confronting the human mind, and that true knowledge consists of the mind's conformity to the reality existing outside of itself. The mind reflects reality, it does not create it. Facts are facts, and it is the mind's task to discern and recognize them.[68]

I reproduce the extended quote because this observation, it seems to me, highlights an essential issue. Do human beings perceive a world that is "out there" in realistic fashion, or does the structure of the human mind pre-arrange the "data"? Baum clarifies the issue by contrasting German philosophy:

> Already Kant insisted that the experience of reality is always mediated through the human mind, that the world out there is never encountered in the raw, and that facts simply as facts are not accessible at all. Contrary to common sense, the reality we encounter, including the facts, is already ordered by the human mind . . . Hegel went much further; for him, the human mind itself was historically constituted. Man's mind was not a given, not identical throughout human history . . . even the structure of the mind . . . was inherited from the particular tradition . . . not only . . . the individual mind [but also] a collective mind, produced by a particular social and cultural tradition . . .[69]

Goethe put it like this:

> Were the eye not attuned to the Sun, The Sun could never be seen by it.[70]

---

[68] Baum, *Religion and Alienation*, 17.
[69] Baum, *Religion and Alienation*, 17.
[70] Quoted by N. R. Hanson as the epigram to his chapter "Observation" in *Patterns of Discovery* (New York: Cambridge University Press, 1958) 4.

Christopher Bryant[71] and Robert N. Proctor[72] profile a series of methodological disputes within German sociology that extended over decades, pivoting around the realist-positivist (O) or subjectivist-hermeneutic (H) issues that Baum outlined. The positivist/subjectivist issue was the topic of a significant symposium as late as 1961 at which critical sociologists of the Frankfurt School (definitely H) squared off against Karl Popper and allies (leaning to O).[73]

In North America, hermeneutical social science appears to have had its start in 1965 when Alvin Gouldner published *Enter Plato*. The book showed that apparently neutral philosophical ideas had their genesis in a society that supported a male leisure class. Knowledge arises in a social setting, after all.[74] But the issues raised by Gouldner and others for North Americans, issues given impetus by Kuhn's new histories of science, had been current for decades in Europe. Troeltsch's early observation of the inevitability of theological assumptions within sociology arose in a long-standing tradition.

With these kinds of limitations, can social scientific work be said to be genuinely scientific? Baum says yes. The results generated by a given researcher may be replicated by another researcher. This is not anecdotal evidence but science. Baum notes, though, that research in sociology is never the same thing as research in the natural sciences. The difference lies in intention, and the interpretation of intention. "Max Weber pointed out that human action consists of behavior plus the meaning the actors assign to it. Since behavior is external, it can be studied with methods similar to those used in the natural sciences. But to study what this behavior means to the actors calls for understanding or interpretation. . . ."[75]

Robin Gill notes that Baum's own orientation is to critical theory. In so placing Baum he locates him somewhat to the left of many theologians. Many theologians who use sociology have opted for a less tenden-

---

[71] Christopher G. A. Bryant, *Positivism in Social Theory and Research* (Basingstoke, Eng.: Macmillan, 1985).

[72] Robert N. Proctor, *Value-Free Science? Purity and Power in Modern Knowledge* (Cambridge: Harvard University Press, 1991).

[73] Adorno et al., *The Positivist Dispute in German Sociology*.

[74] Alvin Gouldner, *Enter Plato: Classical Greece and the Origins of Social Theory* (New York: Basic Books, 1965); Baum, "Remarks of a Theologian," 10. My attribution of Gouldner's leading role for North America comes from Baum and John Coleman. Baum, "The Impact of Sociology on Catholic Theology," in *Theology and Sociology: A Reader*, 132–33; Coleman, "Every Theology Implies a Sociology and Vice Versa," in *Theology and the Social Sciences*, ed. Michael Horace Barnes, 24.

[75] Baum, "Remarks," 7.

tious form of sociology, such as the sociology of Max Weber or of Robert Bellah, a functionalist in the line of Durkheim. Gill says that Baum was much impressed by Karl Mannheim's sociology of knowledge and that Mannheim has influenced Baum's view of the field.[76] In the moral orientation of the critical theorists, Baum detected a resonance with theology's proper concerns.

Baum is conscious of being in a minority. He notes that, in North America at least, sociology in universities and research institutes is still mostly of the scientistic, positivist kind.[77] Baum's account of the majority form of sociology gives additional insight into positivism. He says that positivist sociologists perform empirical research to demonstrate hypotheses purporting to explain some action in society. Once the hypothesis has been established, they make predictions about behavior. Definitely this is Lee's procedure.[78] But, Baum objects, this pattern of research insists on turning qualities into quantities. All qualities are thought to be quantifiable without loss of truth. Baum notes that the first "Scientific Positivists" based their research on "a naïve epistemology" in which the "observing subject gained knowledge of the observed object by gathering quantitative information . . . and . . . constructing a verifiable theory explaining its behavior."[79] This neutral-observer method of gaining sure knowledge has roots in the philosophy of René Descartes (1596–1650). Following the Cartesian method, Sociology "O" sees itself as value-neutral, "unrelated to the personal convictions of the researcher," and hence unrelated to theology. Such neutrality is Lee's view. The "O" approach claims autonomy for the sociology of religion and demands non-interference from theologians committed to a particular religion.[80] Following Descartes's method, knowledge obtained by the method is regarded as objective and universal:[81]

> The positivistic sociologist . . . thinks that the methods devised by him enable him to be in touch with the facts and draw valid conclusions independent of any theory . . . he tries to free his observations from any particular understanding of social development

---

[76] Gill, "Introduction," in *Theology and Sociology: A Reader*, 1–26.

[77] Baum, *Religion and Alienation*, 258, corroborated by Bryant, *Positivism in Social Theory*, 118.

[78] Above, 48. [X-ref]

[79] Baum, *Religion and Alienation*, 115.

[80] Ibid., 259–260.

[81] Ibid., 115.

and from any set of values, hoping thereby to achieve scientific results that are more solidly grounded in reality.[82]

The differences between types "O" and "H" are arguments about the adequacy of bare empiricism. They are not differences of emphasis only. Baum shows that the empirical results produced by social scientists are generated by a wider set of assumptions than they recognize. The problem of positivistic empiricism is not that the facts come without theory. It is that internal connections between fact and interpretation are not noticed.[83] The fact is just "there" as an atheoretical *given*.[84] Type "O" is not frank about its presuppositions.

Type "H," on the other hand, asks about the character of the witness. If the assertion of fact is made, Type "H" asks, "Who says?" Where Type "O's" witness is an abstracted, hidden, or absent observer, Type "H" asks about the fact's observer. Empiricism "O" takes the observer (him or herself, the society of which he or she is part) ideologically as is, without accounting for standpoint or place or interests.[85] Type "H" wishes to recollect the subject. "H" wants no more amnesia. Because subject and object are intertwined, Baum says researchers must determine "the precise place they occupy in this (hermeneutical) circle."[86]

Baum's work begins to show that personal commitments, not omitting theological commitments, necessarily enter into social theorizing. Empirical social scientists are seeing something, surely; numbers are produced from that "something." In some sense empirical data is "scientific." Results can at least be replicated; in surveys or experimental data, the same results can be obtained on a second run of the study. However, results of a given study may well contradict other studies. Contradictions are due to the fact that sight and sense data is human. Humans are subjective observers embedded in cultural-historical contexts.

A religious educator's faith necessarily affects what he or she perceives and prescribes. Coming to faith is scripturally described as coming to see.

---

[82] Baum, "Sociology and Theology," 25.

[83] Bryant, *Positivism in Social Theory,* 3, 4, 142.

[84] Ibid., 3–4.

[85] Karl Mannheim, "Theology and the Sociology of Knowledge," in *Theology and Sociology: A Reader,* 85. The term 'interests' is specifically employed by another critical theorist, Jürgen Habermas, who sees either technical, hermeneutic or emancipatory interests generating knowledge, per Bryant, *Positivism in Social Theory,* 8–9; and also James Loder, *The Transforming Moment: Understanding Convictional Experiences* (San Francisco: Harper & Row, 1981) 28, n. 7.

[86] Baum, "The Impact of Sociology on Catholic Theology," 133.

Jesus employed sight as an epistemological metaphor: "He who sees me sees the one who sent me" (John 12:45).[87] For a religious educator, a non-committed approach will not be acceptable. Anyone who has had a conversion experience will not rest easy with the proposition that the world can be adequately described without reference to the possibility of an alternate way of seeing. Religious education necessarily means educating within a committed worldview, even, within a particular theology. Even if pluralism or the unknowability of truth becomes the driving tenet, still, the unknowability of truth is itself a religious assertion. Further, any faith system will prescribe, or proscribe, particular methods of educating. While it might seem that religious commitment is only in the material that is the "subject," Lee sees that the process is itself a kind of content. If he is right—I agree with him here—then educational process must not contradict the faith commitments of educator and students.

Baum shows that subject and object, observer and observed, fact and interpretation, are intertwined. The significance of fact and value's mutual dependence is developed further in the groundbreaking work of Don Browning.

Don Browning

In *Religious Thought and the Modern Psychotherapies,* Don Browning, professor of divinity at the University of Chicago, uncovers hidden metaphysical and ethical dimensions of modern psychologies.[88] He sheds light also on the way scientific method produces "fact."

Browning's first task is a review of fellow theologians' accounts of psychology. Theologians account for psychology's claims in various ways. Browning reviews the proposals of Paul Tillich, Reinhold Niebuhr, Seward Hiltner, Daniel Day Williams, Malcolm Jeeves, and David Myers. He says that these theologians are really in accord. Their common claim is that "the more narrowly conceived clinical or experimental psychologies simply work at a different level of explanation and for this reason, cannot finally conflict with theological or religious explanations."[89] In this view, psychologies are complementary to theologies and vice versa. Lee, like these older

---

[87] The metaphor extends from Genesis 3:5 "Your eyes will be opened, knowing good and evil" through to Ephesians 1:18 where Paul prays that the eyes of the Ephesians' hearts would be enlightened.

[88] Don S. Browning, *Religious Thought and the Modern Psycho-therapies: A Critical Conversation* (Philadelphia: Fortress, 1987).

[89] Ibid., 14.

theologians, also reconciles social sciences with theology by saying that they operate on different levels.[90]

Browning wishes to challenge the two-level conception. He recognizes that psychologies speak other languages than theology. Taking a cue from Ludwig Wittgenstein, Browning says that psychologies follow distinctive language games.[91] Browning wishes not peaceful co-existence but a true conversation between the disciplines. In order to enable conversation he will expose the "full normative horizon" of the modern psychologies.[92] Browning hopes to uncover where and how the psychologies go beyond their competence by showing that they include ethical and metaphysical dimensions, so as to give voice for theology in dialogue. Browning's method is a revised critical correlation taken from David Tracy, revised and expanded from the correlation method of Tillich. More than being complements to each other, correlated disciplines are to query, clarify or correct each other.

Browning the theologian cross-examines the psychologies by locating extended metaphors that serve as theoretical models. In Lakoff and Johnson's seminal work, metaphor is the organizing principle of scientific theory-building.[93] Metaphors are virtual scaffolds. It is possible that metaphors may be purely scientific in intention, but it is also possible that they go beyond just organizing data. Metaphors may be powerful enough to bear implicit assertions of life's ultimates, the purpose of life. For instance, Lakoff uncovered metaphors of a father-dominant family in the rhetoric of U.S. political conservatives. Uncovering the father metaphor helped to account for what Lakoff, a liberal, had found incomprehensible.[94] A more directly pertinent example for Lee is the way that mechanistic materialism became "a controlling image for reflection on social phenomena" during the latter part of the 19th century, even though it was "originally designed as a metaphor for reflection on phenomena in the physical world."[95] Valuing is already present in the metaphorical scaffold. These themes point

---

[90] Lee, *Shape*, 228; "Authentic Source," 174–92.

[91] Browning, *Religious Thought and the Modern Psychotherapies*, 6.

[92] Ibid., 15.

[93] George Lakoff and Mark Johnson, *Metaphors We Live By* (Chicago: University of Chicago Press, 1980).

[94] George Lakoff, "Metaphor, Morality, and Politics, Or, Why Conservatives Have Left Liberals In the Dust," *Social Research* 62.2 (1995).

[95] Edmund V. Sullivan, *A Critical Psychology: Interpretation of the Personal World* (New York: Plenum, 1984) 3.

to the hopes behind Lee's theorizing. To such a theorist, technical control is good.

Metaphor is not new for religious educators. Duane Huebner and Mary Elizabeth Mullino Moore explored metaphor's role in theorizing.[96] Ruth Poochigian's doctoral dissertation identifies metaphors in Lee of "manipulation, control, prediction, verification, production and measurable outcomes."[97] Following Lakoff's analysis, the metaphor functioning under Lee's terms "manipulation," "control," and so on is "education is production," or "education is science."

Browning traces the ways metaphors function in psychological theory. As sample inquiries, he takes five paradigms of psychology, those of Sigmund Freud, Carl Rogers/Abraham Maslow/Fritz Perls, B. F. Skinner, Carl Jung, and Erik Erikson/Heinz Kohut. Browning succeeds in displaying metaphors of ultimacy within each psychological culture. For instance, the Oedipal myth functions as a metaphor of ultimacy for Freudians. Freudians carry on Freud's commitment to ethical reciprocity and disavowal of the Western tradition of agape love. Browning finds that the psychologies are indeed theorized by ultimate metaphors. As he is able to show "metaphors of ultimacy" within the psychologies, he displays propositions about cosmology, about the way things are in the universe, about ontology, elements that are worldview or metaphysical in nature. Thus he reminds us that "decisions about the metaphors we use to represent the ultimate context of experience are first a matter of faith."[98] When they travel beyond their allotted bounds, Browning says that psychologies ought to offer an account.

Isolating metaphor's role in Lee illumines his conception of method. Lee's method is a scientific method, of course. The scientific method is the method that produces sure and certain fact by observation, prediction and verification. As one theologian outlines matters, "The establishment of facts implies a scientific method. The process is first inductive; one gathers data and generalizes to hypotheses. Then one 'derives predictions and discards unconfirmed hypotheses.'"[99] The establishing of fact springs from an underlying philosophy of science. From Baum we saw that basic philosophical issues are not somehow bypassed when a human observer

---

[96] Duane Huebner, "Religious Metaphors in the Language of Education," *Religious Education* 80 (1985) 460–71; Mary Elizabeth Mullino Moore, *Teaching from the Heart: Theology and Educational Method* (Minneapolis: Fortress, 1991).

[97] Ruth L. Poochigian, "Critical Analysis," 116.

[98] Browning, *Religious Thought and the Modern Psychotherapies*, 59.

[99] Poythress, *Science and Hermeneutics*, 36.

claims to have observed a subject. A philosophical assertion is implicitly being made when a phenomenon is said to be a "fact." Descartes's pursuit of sure and certain knowledge found expression in his philosophy.[100] His philosophy was foundational for the method. Descartes, incidentally, was an innovator: Walter Ong says that until the sixteenth century "there was no word in ordinary usage which clearly expressed what we mean today by "method," a series of ordered steps gone through to produce with certain efficacy a desired effect—a routine of efficiency."[101]

The discovery that theory in science has a metaphorical structure raises three issues for educators. First, metaphor in theory means that values intrude into scientific theorizing. Second, the science appropriate to human subjects becomes a question once again. Third, metaphor in theory raises the question of appropriate methodology for religious educational research.

First, metaphor-structured theory means that values do work in theorizing that seems to be value-neutral. Lakoff and Johnson illustrate this reality when they point out that in Western cultures we tend to talk about argument as warfare. "We can actually *win* or *lose* arguments. We see the person we are arguing with as an *opponent*. We *attack* his decisions and defend our own. We *gain* and *lose* ground. We plan and use *strategies* . . ."[102] Lakoff asks how we would perceive argument differently were "argument is dance" the controlling metaphor. "Argument is dance" would project expectations of co-operation for a beauty that left participants and onlookers satisfied.

D. I. Smith summarizes linguistic and educational theorists to note that metaphors form "storehouses of expectation" that shape what teachers "expect from themselves and what they expect others to expect from them."[103] A course of action is preferred over another because it fits with the structural metaphor. Smith analyses Comenius's use of the garden image for educational development. Comenius's gardening metaphor is able to suggest service of God and others rather than "exploitative mastery."[104]

---

[100] I owe the basic insight to Dr. Robert Knudsen, my seminary instructor in philosophy of science. Also Elliot Eisner, *Educational Imagination,* 46, quoted above.

[101] Walter Ong, *Ramus: Method, and the Decay of Dialogue: From the Art of Discourse to the Art of Reason* (Cambridge: Harvard University Press, 1958) 225, cited in David I. Smith, "Modern Language Pedagogy, Spiritual Development and Christian Faith: A Study of Their Interrelationships" (Ph.D. diss., University of London, 2000) 92–132.

[102] Lakoff and Johnson, *Metaphors We Live By.*

[103] Smith, "Modern Language Pedagogy," 92–132.

[104] Ibid.

"Education in a classroom conceived as a factory and one viewed as a garden . . . is likely to differ."[105] This exposition illustrates the way that values find a place in educational theory via metaphor. Lee's metaphors of control import his values of what it is to be truly human.

Second, the uncovering of metaphor raises new caution about appropriate scientific methods for human subjects. The propriety of a scientific method originally for unconscious physical phenomena but applied to human subjects has been disputed since the advent of the social sciences, in the 1800s. A sizable literature exists on the historical development of social sciences, and earlier debates cast light on recurrent issues. Dorothy Ross traces how the earliest sociologists in America thought it possible to include moral dimensions in social science. Their concerns, however, were sidelined by a generation that wished physical science rigor and prestige for their discipline.[106] Natural science will be reductionistic as to what it cannot observe; to notice the reduction is to notice a profound deficit.[107] Lee opted for a scientific method that systematically overlooks aspects of humanness.

Third, the uncovering of metaphor in theory raises the question of an appropriate methodology for religious educational research. I use the word "methodology" here intending a broader meaning than "method"; "method" connotes Ong's precise series of ordered steps. Lee presents his favored research as privileged, somehow "harder" than rivals. Possibly, a procedure that seems looser will take in more of the variables of religious education.[108] Edmund Sullivan, for instance, suggests that "the paradigm of the personal world is communication itself." Following Paul Ricoeur, Sullivan suggests that meaningful action itself be considered a text. If it is human action we wish to interpret, "mechanical and organic

---

[105] Ibid.

[106] Dorothy Ross, "The Development of the Social Sciences," in *The Organization of Knowledge in Modern America, 1860–1920,* ed. Alexandra Oleson and John Voss (Baltimore and London: Johns Hopkins University Press, 1979); also Julie A. Reuben, *The Making of the Modern University: Intellectual Transformation and the Marginalization of Morality* (Chicago: University of Chicago Press, 1996).

[107] Ray S. Anderson, *On Being Human: Essays in Theological Anthropology* (Grand Rapids: Eerdmans, 1982) 13.

[108] See Joseph Dunne's *Back to the Rough Ground: Practical Judgment and the Lure of Technique* (Notre Dame: University of Notre Dame Press, 1993) for his rehabilitation of phronesis, the practical knowledge directed toward virtue, against long-dominant techne or technical rationality, 8–10. Five kinds of rationality, not just one, are profiled by Richard Osmer, "Rationality in Practical Theology," *International Journal of Practical Theology* 1 (1997) 11–40. Dunne relates the analysis directly to education, 377–79.

metaphors" are at a significant disadvantage to a personal metaphor.[109] Aspects of Sullivan's critical methodology are echoed in the work of Joseph Dunne and in D. I. Smith's explorations toward a faith-consistent second-language pedagogy.[110] I offer the above to suggest that alternative systematic "scientific" procedures—methodologies—for education research already exist. Of course, alternative methodologies have existed: anthropological explorations such as Geertz's "thick description" have been employed in schools of education for decades. What is new in scholars like Dunne or Smith is a denial that empiricism can be just another perspective along with other research findings. The affirmation of Dunne or Smith, not to mention Ricoeur or Sullivan, is that empiricism bears with it undeclared commitments that are metaphysical in nature. Before true conversation can commence the metaphysical commitments must be acknowledged.

Browning asserts in numerous places that the contributions of the psychologies, the basic insights, their way of seeing, are here to stay. His desire is not to eliminate the psychologies but to require them to acknowledge their ethical freight. He wants to set out their ethical and metaphysical claims for inspection, to facilitate wise use. If psychologies do carry religious implications, let them be examined and critiqued by those whose primary commitment is to, say, a Jewish or Christian tradition. "Rather than asking the psychologists . . . to suppress their moral commitments or their deep metaphors, one would ask instead that they be brought to the surface, critically tested, and replaced if they appear inadequate."[111]

Browning helps educators toward a possible accounting of what is unacknowledged in positivistic social science. Browning displays how a particular social science, psychology, is inherently normative. His study shows that, despite pretensions to scientific neutrality, the psychologies are metaphysically dependent. When a social science appears to possess authority from its value-freedom, neutrality, and objectivity, such an appearance is a pretension. Theologians must appropriate a psychology critically.

However, while Browning recognizes that it is difficult for psychologies not to have normative aspects to their theorizing,[112] he does not rule

---

[109] Sullivan, *A Critical Psychology*, 111.

[110] Dunne, *Back to the Rough Ground*; D. I. Smith, "Modern Language Pedagogy"; also "Christian Thinking in Education Reconsidered," *Spectrum* 27.1 (1995) 1–17, and "The Curious Idea of a Christian Teaching Method," keynote address at the Eighth Annual Conference of the North American Christian Foreign Language Association, Anderson University, Anderson, Indiana, March 25-27, 1999.

[111] Browning, *Religious Thought and the Modern Psychotherapies*, 242.

[112] Ibid., 60.

out the possibility of neutral empirical fact. Browning wants theology to have its due, and he wants the psychologies to have their due. The psychologies are not to cross the line. The psychologies, per Browning, can come so far, but no further. Psychologies may make less-than-ultimate assertions, but not ultimate ones. They can make assertions within a scientific sandbox, as it were, but not beyond it. Browning admits that "prior critical and normative understandings of the dialectical relation between the good person and the good society" are essential to many foundational psychological tasks, such as describing identity.[113] At the same time he says that ultimate organizing principles, the models, the metaphors, are metaphysical, possibly theological. He may not be recognizing that the structuring or "deep" metaphors themselves can have a role in generating "facts." If we know from him that psychologies require an ultimate explaining metaphor in order to function, are the psychologies not serving as, so to speak, street-level retailers of particular metaphysical commitments? Deprived of their organizing principle, no longer will they be able to explain what they see. An unexplained phenomenon can hardly be truly observed.[114] A minimal implication of Browning's analysis is that a committed educator requires not a neutral psychology but a psychology reworked to be consistent with his or her commitments. Empirical social science acknowledging its metaphysical and critical corollaries would be one step in an honest direction.

It is questionable that an autonomous psychology is possible. The psychologies are more committed to their worldview than even Browning recognizes. Since the Kuhnian revolution, since Gouldner and the hermeneutical turn, since Derrida, Michel Foucault and postmodernism, the possibility of an empiricism that is de-ethicized, de-normed, or shorn of its metaphysical side is increasingly problematic.

Recall now that Lee says,

> By use of carefully constructed methodological controls, social science can free itself from the inevitable tilt of the personal subjective judgment of researcher and so can attain a more or less objective approximation of the personal and/or social phenomenon under investigation.[115]

---

[113] Ibid., 242–43.

[114] For instance, George Lindbeck critiques a false dualism of experience and interpretation in *The Nature of Doctrine: Religion and Theology in a Postliberal Age* (Philadelphia: Fortress, 1983) as also Francis Schüssler Fiorenza, *Foundational Theology: Jesus and the Church* (New York: Crossroad, 1984) esp. 297–98.

[115] Lee, "Social Science," 599.

Even more specifically,

> Value-freedom in social science means, among other things, that (1) social science is not normative with respect to religious and moral values; hence social science cannot state what ought to be religiously or morally; (2) social science of itself cannot assign moral or religious value to any reality; (3) social science can deal with a wide variety of morally and religiously value-laden areas without having to necessarily express a preference for one another [sic] value based on the intrinsic moral and religious merits of that value.[116]

I repeat Lee verbatim in the context of Browning so readers see that Lee's empirical social science is subject to significant qualification. Empiricism's dominance led to questions of sufficient depth that rival social sciences were conceived. Lee's social science religious instruction cannot be the sole macrotheory for educating in religion.

John Milbank

The third theologian of the social sciences for our study of Lee is John Milbank. Milbank's *Theology and Social Theory* gained considerable attention after it was published in 1990, winning its author notice in the *Chronicle of Higher Education, Christian Century,* and other publications. Milbank's project in *Theology and Social Theory* is to uncover the metaphysical foundations of social theory. He proceeds by an archeology of sociological theory per se, delving into the philosophy that made a discourse called "sociology" possible. He demonstrates that social "sciences" are founded on tacit philosophical-theological assumptions. Milbank claims,

> ... secular discourse does not just "borrow" inherently inappropriate modes of expression from religion as the only discourse to hand ... but is actually *constituted* in its secularity by "heresy" in relation to orthodox Christianity, or else a rejection of Christianity that is more "neo-pagan" than simply anti-religious.[117]

Milbank's philosophical detective work adds significantly to my analysis of Lee's social science instruction theory. I limit myself to his genetic account of sociology's origins. The origins show metaphysical and ethical foundations of the social sciences that continue to the present.

---

[116] Lee, "Authentic Source," 132–33.

[117] Milbank, *Theology and Social Theory: Beyond Secular Reason* (Oxford: Blackwell, 1990) 3, emphasis his.

Milbank's genealogy traces sociology to the attempt of Catholic theorists after the French Revolution to locate a new basis for society. The theorists Louis de Bonald, Joseph de Maistre, and Claude Henri de St. Simon preceded Auguste Comte, usually said to be the father of sociology, by a decade or more. Milbank's tracing of the founding concepts of sociology reworks Robert Nisbet[118] and Anthony Giddens.[119] Nisbet and Giddens recognized the Catholic counter-revolutionaries but thought that social theory was a child of Enlightenment philosophy. Milbank's detective work goes further back. The opening paragraph of his book begins the story:

> Once, there was no "secular." And the secular was not latent, waiting to fill more space with the steam of the "purely human" when the pressure of the sacred was relaxed. Instead there was the single community of Christendom, with its dual aspects of *sacerdotium* and *regnum*. The *saeculum*, in the medieval era, was not a space, a domain, but a time—the interval between fall and *eschaton* where coercive justice, private property and impaired natural reason must make shift to cope with the unredeemed effects of sinful humanity.[120]

Seen within orthodox Christianity's understanding of the immanent-transcendent God in relation to the world, "secular" is a construction. The idea of secularity acquired growing cultural persuasiveness within a set of historical circumstances. "Once, there was no 'secular'." Specific philosophical-theological moves made it possible for European civilization to imagine a sphere of action independent of God and the church.

Milbank finds the basic moves of sociology in pre-Enlightenment theological, political and legal theory. Political theorists such as Grotius and Hobbes articulated views of the state as a legal personage. The state was formed by natural rights surrendered by free individuals. Natural law was taken to be transparent for all observers. Just as it is natural for a creature to arrange for self preservation, so states were said, naturally, to be concerned for self preservation. The understanding of legitimate "needs" in this way was stretched from creation to human living. Milbank says, "Grotius, Hobbes and Spinoza can be confident that the self-preserving

---

[118] Robert Nisbet, *The Sociological Tradition* (London: Heinemann, 1966) cited in Milbank, *Theology and Social Theory*, 71, n. 1.

[119] Anthony Giddens, "Four Myths in the History of Social Thought," in *Studies in Social and Political Theory* (New York: Basic Books, 1977), cited in Milbank, *Theology and Social Theory*, 71, n. 2.

[120] Milbank, *Theology and Social Theory*, 9, emphasis his. The citations in brackets that follow are from this work.

conatus provides the universal hermeneutic key for both nature and society" (10). Another key move is that the old Roman view of household *dominium,* where the father has all rights over his home and possessions, moves from the fringe into the center of political theory (12). These moves served to construct the state in a way that was and is free from "suggestions of collective essence or generally recognized *telos*" (13).

Another piece of the puzzle is how such developments could "ever secure legitimacy in a theological and metaphysical era" (14). The answer is that components of the secular shift were in fact "theologically promoted" (14). Ontology or metaphysics had developed significantly in the later middle ages. "*Dominium,* as power, could only become the human essence, because it was seen as reflecting the divine essence, a radical divine simplicity without real or formal differentiation" (14). If human beings are recognized as bearing the image of God, and God is essentially about will or power, then human beings must be about will or power also. Theology affirmed that humans came closest to the image of God when enjoying unrestricted property rights and "even more when exercising the rights of a sovereignty that 'cannot bind itself'" (15). It also abandoned participation in the being and unity of God, the older basis for human interrelationships, in favor of relationships as contractual (15). The late-medieval shift in trinitarian theology opened up space for newly "secular" views of humanness.

> In the thought of the nominalists, following Duns Scotus, the Trinity loses its significance as a prime location for discussing will and understanding in God and the relationship of God to the world. No longer is the world participatorily enfolded within the divine expressive *logos,* but instead a bare divine unity starkly confronts the other distinct unities which he has ordained (14).

God is arbitrary in power and action. Milbank is able to trace this conception forward to Hobbes, who declares in unmistakable theological language, "The right of Nature, whereby God reigneth over men . . . is to be derived, not from his creating them, as if he required obedience as of gratitude for his benefits; but from his *Irresistible Power.*"[121] Thus theology created the space for the first social science, secularized political theory.

Milbank confirms his analysis by noting even earlier parallel developments within the church—in canon law, or in sub-Christian theorists such as Machiavelli. However, it is outside our purpose to follow Milbank

---

[121] Milbank, *Theology and Social Theory,* 15, quoting Hobbes, *Leviathan,* pt. 2, ch. 31 (Harmondsworth, Eng.: Penguin, 1968) 397.

on those paths. The point of this limited treatment is that the moves that made secularism possible were not necessary, essential, or inescapable. Developments within intellectual history opened up the possibility of the discourse that became social science. Contingent developments made social scientific discourse plausible. Those developments included—most definitely—theological affirmations of a metaphysical character. Affirmations in nominalism made the character or nature of God to be absolute. It seems ironic that these affirmations open up the possibility of a free space for human to act independently of this absolutist God, yet that development is precisely what Milbank traced. One could imagine other scholars giving other accounts of the rise of modernity. Disputes over the philosophy and theology implicit in modernity's development would seem probable. However, Milbank is a pioneer in tracing the genealogy of political and social theory to metaphysical assumptions. Presuppositions that Michael Polanyi more generally terms "tacit," Milbank locates and names.

The value of Milbank for understanding Lee's theory is that Milbank corroborates and extends what we have already seen in Baum and Browning. Fact is not neutral; it is theory dependent. Fact's dependence on theory includes understandings of God, self, and world: the nature of reality.

Lee's Social Science

Lee acknowledges that what counts as social science remains "controverted," some distinguishing "social sciences, the semisocial sciences, and the sciences with social implications. . . . "[122] However, to my knowledge Lee never writes in the perspective of a particular psychological school or in the perspective of a particular sociologist, represented as a particular school of thought. The many studies used in *The Flow of Religious Instruction* are from educational research, as are his citations generally, plus psychological studies or sociology. Lee registers admiration for Jung's psychological theory, for instance, but he never registers that the school of interpretation bears on what counts as empirical fact. Lee's concern is for bare empirical data. He has the highest respect for tested observation.[123]

One of Lee's examples clarifies what he sees as the advantage of empirical observation over theology:

> . . . there has been dispute among theologians throughout the centuries as to the most propitious moment for first communion . . . The duration of this theological dispute and the variegation of

---

[122] Lee, *Shape*, 134.
[123] Lee, *Shape*, 136.

opinions serve as an indication that a real solution to this question is not within the scope of theological science. Social-science investigation can reveal the *actual facts* of the psychological maturation, readiness, and development of children of different age levels, together with the kinds of interactions they have with parents and peer group members. On this basis, a decision can be intelligently made. . . . [124]

Notice several aspects of this quote. First, social science reveals what it reveals in neutral fashion. Social science is taken as independent of observer bias. Social science will reveal the "actual facts" about child development, pure and simple. That the child is situated in a society with its own particular set of ideals for childhood and adulthood, variable from culture to culture, is not registered. Lee never admits bias. He includes assumptions about mature human being, the most authentic humanness. These assumptions are already present in the observation act but are not registered.

Second, notice the lack of confidence in theology. There is no doubt that disputes about the timing of first communion—and even bigger topics—have served to reduce confidence in theology.[125] But it is more and more questionable that metaphysical commitments are bypassed by simply "looking and seeing."

Lee's positive attitude to empirical observation clearly owes something significant to his theological immanentism. Indeed, his affirmation of social science stands on immanentism. A religious person would say that observed facts just "are," only by stressing that God is at work throughout creation and all facts indiscriminately are God's facts. Lee says that social science does not uncover "ultimate nature or ultimate functions"; rather, social science deals with those which can be uncovered by observation. These natures or functions are proximate, not ultimate.[126] But no contradiction between this proximate world and ultimate reality is considered. Ultimate reality is inaccessible to observation, but the "mysterious is not inaccessible" because human and empirical results are manifested in the world of sight and sense.[127] In this depiction, proximate creation and humanity are in harmony with ultimate reality. The world is not askew. The epistemology of Lee's theory in this chapter proves to be interrelated with

---

[124] Lee, *Shape*, 136.
[125] Vern S. Poythress, *Science and Hermeneutics,* 20–21.
[126] Lee, "Social science," 598.
[127] Lee, *Flow,* 295.

its theological aspects in the next chapter. I reserve theological considerations mainly for Chapter 3, where an assessment of Lee's immanence theology is found. My point for now is that Lee's empiricism and immanentism are linked.

From the discussion, I label Lee a sacramental positivist. Recall the quote: "If sacramental theory is incorporated within . . . personality theory, and allowed free rein to interact with the various facts and laws . . . then religious instruction has achieved that congenial fruitful working relationship between theology and social science."[128] For Lee, the historical incarnation of God in Jesus Christ baptized all of reality, so social phenomena can be measured without second thought. "The very Incarnation event itself bears supreme witness that the concrete reigns over the abstract for those of us here on earth."[129] Lee sees the whole of reality without differentiation and therefore gives a blessing to virtually all social science.

Lee is not the first sacramental positivist. Kolakowski gives instances from late medieval nominalism. Nominalism is the denial of the reality of universal classes except as names; kinds or genres have no independent reality. Nominalism wished to place faith in its proper sphere. Faith became abstracted to a God whose will appeared as remote and arbitrary. Reason operated on what is seen, on phenomena. Within this milieu, Roger Bacon, (c. 1214–c. 1293) was an early empiricist. Bacon wanted knowledge to be verified by practice. Bacon's "empirical bent extended even into his religious life: he attached an especially high value to mystical experience, as a means of direct communication with the divine source of being."[130] His positivism arose from distinctive theological conceptions. Lee has a mystical side also which will appear in the discussion of cognition and language in Chapter 3.

The argument is, again, that Lee's theory may not be taken as a macrotheory for all religious instruction because it relies on particular theological affirmations. This chapter showed that both philosophies of science and theology's analysis of its relation to social sciences now dis avow neutrality in the human sciences. I showed that "social science" necessarily includes metaphysical underpinnings. Attempting to portray themselves as scientific and neutral, empirical social scientists have been less than frank about their metaphysics. But neutrality has been shown to be false, especially since Thomas Kuhn. Like other empiricisms, Lee's em-

---

[128] Lee, *Shape*, 245.
[129] Lee, *Shape*, 248.
[130] Kolakowski, Positivist Philosophy, 22.

piricism is metaphysically committed. Lee believes that "scientific" theory must be theologically neutral. Social science religious instruction, however, rests on a demonstrable theology. It must fail as religious instruction's "macrotheory."

3

The Theology of James Michael Lee

THIS chapter confirms that social science religious instruction need not be taken as a macrotheory for the field. Lee's social science religious instruction is based on assumptions. Lee would not have devoted significant segments in the trilogy's prolegomena, *The Shape of Religious Instruction*, to a modernized understanding of revelation had he not been somehow aware of theology's pivotal role. Nor otherwise would he have argued so vigorously with advocates of the "blow theory" of direct divine action.[1] Theological commitments are pilings for Lee's educational superstructure.

Françoise Darcy-Bérubé was the first to publicly issue a challenge to Lee to account for his theology. Darcy-Bérubé said 25 years ago:

> I would insist on the importance of bringing into light and clearly expressing the underlying theology that inspires and shapes both the behavioral outcomes the theory strives to facilitate and, indirectly, the pedagogical means or strategies it proposes . . . It would be very important for Jim to spell out clearly the vision of man, of God, of Church, and of Christian life that inspires his theory.[2]

I accept Darcy-Bérubé's challenge to clarify Lee's theology. Lee's theory is an educational-theological paradigm. His affirmations raise theological issues that have been in dispute for centuries. There is a mainstream view of the issues, and Lee is a variation. But I could not attempt to examine all possible social science religious instruction proposals. Since more than one variety of social science exists, a proposal based on, say, a hermeneutical social science might be possible. We are here concerned with Lee's proposal.

---

[1] Lee, *Flow*, 174–80 is typical.
[2] Darcy-Berube, "The Challenge Ahead of Us," 117.

The aim of this investigation is not to conduct a trial; it is to untangle a genealogy. This chapter is an exercise in understanding. Lee presents his theory as theologically neutral. Other educators see the contrary, that theology is unavoidable. The need of the Christian and religious education field is to see how religious instruction methods relate to theology.

Any Christian theologian writes from a perspective. Lee is a Roman Catholic, and what he takes for granted, a Protestant might overlook. I ask indulgence if I miss undertones that a Catholic would hear naturally.

Lee's Theology of Faith

Lee understands that "faith" is a central concept for his theory. Among other writings, he edited a *Handbook of Faith* to which he contributed an introduction and chapter.[3]

An analyst is immediately confronted with a difficulty. "Faith" is difficult to define. The underlying terms in the Christian scriptures signify reliance on God or a definable body of affirmations called "the faith." Having "faith" must have something to do with "the faith"—the same word is employed.[4] Theologians and creeds affirm a range of meanings too. Faith may be broadly "a central theological concept representing the correct relationship to God."[5] A dictionary article by Craig Dykstra has faith in relation to belief, to action, and to discernment or truth.[6] A summary exposition by Karl Barth has chapters for faith as trust, faith as knowledge, and faith as confession.[7] We are obliged to focus on Lee's precise claims for "faith," while remaining alert to wider perspectives when "faith" is seen more broadly.

Lee defines faith operationally. He limits faith to resulting behaviors. His notion of religion is the functions it performs. Lee defines faith, for practical purposes, as its fruit. Lee's approach is quickly seen: "One reason for the relative ineffectiveness of contemporary religious instruction is the vagueness of its intended objectives. If the objectives are vague, it is difficult for learners to know exactly what they are to learn." Anticipating an objection, Lee continues,

---

[3] Lee, *Handbook of Faith* (Birmingham, Ala: Religious Education Press, 1990); "Introduction," vii-xii; "Facilitating Growth in Faith through Religious Instruction," 264–302.

[4] *Eerdmans Dictionary of the Bible*, s.v. "Faith," ed. D. N. Freedman (Grand Rapids: Eerdmans, 2000); Mary C. Boys, *Educating in Faith*, 4.

[5] *Eerdmans Dictionary of the Bible*, s.v. "Faith."

[6] *Harper's Encyclopedia of Religious Education*, s.v. "Faith."

[7] Barth, *Dogmatics in Outline* (New York: Harper & Brothers, 1959) 15–34.

> The supernatural element in religious instruction introduces a new and strong variable which at first blush would seem to place a difficult if not insuperable obstacle in the path of both operationalizing the objectives of religious instruction and of building a taxonomy of instructional objectives for the religious domain . . . One way out of the apparent problem posed for religious instruction by theologians is to view religion operationally.[8]

Lee deals with the obvious objection this way:

> . . . some religious educators advance the fallacious argument that religious dimensions of teaching and learning are inaccessible to scientific investigation, and that the social-science approach is therefore inadequate for religion teaching. This argument fails because it ignores the very obvious fact that religion is a human phenomenon and therefore is amenable to empirical as well as to nonempirical investigation.[9]

Lee is certainly correct that "religious" phenomena are measurable. One society may be compared with another in all kinds of ways, including religious. But "religion" is slippery, referring now to a complex of beliefs plus consistent and inconsistent behavior of a group, and alternately to the acquisition of religious sensibility. Where a society will yield measurement readily, measurement of personal sensibility will be inferential, not direct. Lee would likely dismiss a distinction. Fruit, or visible results, is to him the only way of assessing religiosity. If "it" cannot be assessed, then "it" is not relevant. In the words of the quotation above, religion is indeed a human phenomenon and amenable to investigation—but it may not be limited to the empirical. If Lee responded that he nowhere limits the study of religion to empirical investigation, the claim would be accurate enough; he recognizes complementary perspectives.[10] But the crucial point is that only the empirical is allowed a place for religious instruction theory. For the theory, faith is its fruits. His orientation to visible effects is seen here:

> I am not suggesting that social science provides the entire framework for religious instruction. To be sure, the work of the supernatural constitutes a central variable in the enterprise of religious instruction. However, the supernatural cannot be measured by empirical procedures. Indeed, theological science itself seems hard pressed to make any sort of accurate assessment of the supernatural

---

[8] Lee, *Shape*, 69, also *Flow*, 23, 196, 276.

[9] Lee, *Flow*, 295; "Authentic Source," 104, 106.

[10] See Ch. 2. p. 21, n. 28, n. 29 [x-refs].

> effects of religious instruction. But the evaluation and improvement of a particular religion class or religion curriculum are dependent upon the degree to which the learner's behavior is being modified along desired religious lines. . . . It is proper to assume, I think, that an increase in faith and charity and other supernatural virtues will cause a related change in the religious behavior of the learner to the extent that he has acquired one or more of these supernatural qualities.[11]

The extended quotation is necessary so the reader may notice a change of subject. "But," seen in the middle of the paragraph, indicates an abrupt ending of discourse on the ineffable quality of "supernatural effects." Lee can go no further with the supernatural. He returns to his base line: he stipulates that outward religious change will mirror inward religious change. He says that evaluation of religious instruction depends "upon the degree" of behavior change. Inward change is "to the extent" that behaviors are demonstrated. If "it" cannot be seen, "it" may be practically dismissed.

Lee calls faith a "construct"—an "abstraction formed by making a generalization from a body of particulars."[12] "Faith" is the name of a set of behaviors. Thus "faith must be teachable, since all behaviors are teachable."[13] The emphasis is not new; Lee said in 1977, "Christian doctrine is an operationalized pattern of life. Christian doctrine in its authentic form is Christian living."[14]

Limiting faith to behaviors is a key move that makes a social science approach to instruction possible. Unless transcendent, theological, or miraculous factors are minimized, an immanent social science approach to instruction could not work. A set of uncontrollable variables or unknowns would exist. To Lee, the teaching of religion has been vague in objective and the task frustrated. Unknowns hamstrung religious development. His approach is to specify behavioral goals and reconfigure the unknowns of instruction as (immanent) knowns. Accordingly, empirical research appears to provide direction to religious instruction because Lee's objectives are unreasonably narrow. Faith is just behaviors. Lee, like a behaviorist, overlooks motivation.

---

[11] Lee, *Shape*, 188–89.

[12] Lee, "Authentic Source," 106, "Facilitating Growth," 271. Note that this way of speaking is nominalist, as against the realist tradition. The classes or categories are invented, arbitrary 'names' or 'constructs'.

[13] Lee, "Facilitating Growth," 270.

[14] Lee, "Toward a New Era: A Blueprint for Positive Action," 126.

Faith identified as its visible result, cause matched to effect only, fits precisely with Lee's view of teaching related to learning. "The basic nature of religious instruction is properly described in terms of the causation of desired learning outcomes. If learning outcomes have not occurred, then there has been no religious instruction, no matter how holy or how theologically erudite the religious educator is."[15] Faith equals its visible results, and this ties perfectly to the educational affirmation. "A social science-based theory of religious instruction . . . holds that the significant variables which explain, predict, and verify the process of teaching religion are *those involved in the effective modification* of the learner's behavior along religious lines."[16]

We may now locate Lee in a spectrum of possible definitions of faith. *The New Dictionary of Theology* observes, "Both Scripture and the church traditions (Catholic and Protestant) appear to say that faith is mysteriously both a divine gift and an uncoerced human activity." It continues, "some theologians lay more stress on the human factors leading to conviction about God and Christ, while others suggest that such conviction is wholly or primarily the result of a unique operation of the Holy Spirit in human hearts." Lee's stress may be one-sided but is not unprecedented. A clue to the history of the issue lies in the dictionary's opening statement: "The relationship between our freedom to repent and to believe in Christ, on the one hand, and the giving of repentance and faith, on the other, has been a matter of contention among Christians since the days of Augustine in the 5th century."[17] Lee is aware that divergent opinion exists. He opposes his operational definition of religion with a notional one. For a notional definition he cites L. de Grandmaison who said that "Religion is the relationship of man, individually and collectively, with God."[18] Defending the

---

[15] Lee, "Authentic Source," 127.

[16] Lee, "Authentic Source," 135, emphasis mine.

[17] *New Dictionary of Theology* s.v. "Faith," eds. S. B. Ferguson and D.F. Wright (Leicester: InterVarsity, 1988).

[18] Lee, "Facilitating Growth," 272–73. The notional definition of 'religion' is similar to the *New Dictionary of Theology*'s 'faith' quoted above. Lee says in the introduction to the *Handbook of Faith* (1990), "Whether one regards faith as the central category of human existence . . . or . . . love . . . as . . . other religionists like myself do . . . faith is an extraordinarily important construct in religion" (vii). The terms 'religion' and 'faith' are slippery and include between them substantial semantic overlap. Contemporary Protestants make little use of 'religion' as in the older "he got religion" and seem to prefer e.g. 'having faith' or 'coming to faith'. But this usage of 'faith' is similar to a Catholic 'religion,' something that may be possessed and exercised. In Lee's usage 'religion' and 'faith' are closely related; see his definition of religion in "Authentic Source" 100.

priority of the operational definition, Lee writes, "the issue is not whether God works intrinsically in man or in the teaching-learning dynamic, but how he works."[19] Lee takes the (to him) true and only genuinely defensible stand.[20]

In a couple of places, Lee attempts to dispense with possible objections to his theory. In *Flow* he denies that his "approach in any way hint[s] that human nature is totally good in itself or is free from taint of original sin in whatever form this sin may be considered." No party with a particular view on original sin could be offended. He lists Pelagians, Augustinians, Thomists, and Jansenists, all with strong views on original sin. All would find social science religious instruction entirely compatible, according to him. The reason is that social science religious instruction goes with any theology; social science is atheological to Lee.[21] In 1990 Lee again notes, "The third objection is that any claim that religious instruction gives rise directly to faith is Pelagianism."[22]

"Pelagian" is not a term that I found in published reactions to Lee. While it may never have appeared in print, it may have been one that Lee overheard or had addressed to him. The apparent charge of "Pelagianism" is a clue for our analysis of Lee's faith.

Pelagianism originated with Pelagius, a British lay ascetic who lived in Rome at the end of the fourth century. Pelagius's concern was for holy living. He believed that the prevailing stress on divine initiative severed the nerve of human responsibility for increased holiness. If human beings are so sunk in sin as to be unable to progress in Christian living without divine action, personal effort and self discipline are pointless. Pelagius's concern parallels Lee's dismay at over-spiritualized education.

Though Pelagius appeared to have support from long-accepted authorities, his stress on human ability ran afoul of an influential bishop in North Africa, Augustine of Hippo. Augustine's replies, derived from scripture, the tradition, and his own experience, urged dependence on divine action. A tendency toward self-will and pride termed original sin means that progress in consistent Christian living requires dependence upon God. Original sin is an inborn tendency acquired from the first human parents, hence, from the origins.[23] Faith as personal trust is pivotal to

---

[19] Lee, *Flow*, 292.
[20] Lee, *Flow*, 47, and endnote 22.
[21] Lee, *Flow*, 292.
[22] Lee, "Facilitating Growth," 271.
[23] The doctrine sounds unmodern, but see H. Blocher's *Original Sin: Illuminating the*

growth in outward religious behaviors. Religious behaviors are not themselves religion.

The controversy ran in print and in official church meetings for some years. Pelagius desisted, but the war continued between the Pelagians Celestius and Julius, a bishop in southern Italy, on one side and Augustine and supporters on the other. While the Pelagians won or drew at two synods in the eastern Mediterranean in 415, ultimately Augustine's party prevailed with the result that a version of Augustinian teaching became the ecclesial standard.[24] But the controversy continued to revive, with Gottschalk in the ninth century, Calvin in the sixteenth, Jansen in the seventeenth and Wesley in the eighteenth. In each recurrence the broad issue was how God's necessary action (the terminology included "grace" or "predestination") is related to human ability, which is more free, less free, or not free.

Lee would not make a distinction between God's action outside nature and within nature. God works proximately, through nature or humanity. A Lee who distinguished divine action from human action would be, on the Augustinian-Pelagian spectrum, on the side of human ability. But Lee's folding of transcendence into immanence seems to alter the analysis. Does the human will the behavior, or is it God? Lee says God works through the here-and-now. The human being wills and acts—that is faith. Faith is a construct. Because faith as dependence has been eliminated, the only God to appeal to is the God who is revealing himself by the actor's own actions. Even prayer is a willed action, and for Lee prayer must be to the God within oneself.[25]

The recurrent Augustinian-Pelagian debate makes clear that Lee's faith is at the human initiative end of the spectrum. Lee requires faith to be immanent and human so it can be manipulated. Otherwise it becomes unscientific.

Riddle (Grand Rapids: Eerdmans, 1997); or Cornelius Plantinga, *Not the Way It's Supposed to Be: A Breviary of Sin* (Grand Rapids: Eerdmans, 1994).

[24] My thumbnail sketch is drawn from J. Pelikan, *The Christian Tradition*, Vol. 1: *The Emergence of the Catholic Tradition (100–600)* (Chicago: University of Chicago Press, 1971); L. Duchesne, *Early History of the Christian Church: From its Foundation to the End of the Fifth Century*, Vol. 3: *The Fifth Century*, trans C. Jenkins (London: John Murray, 1924); H. Chadwick, *Augustine*, in Past Masters series, gen. ed. K. Thomas (Oxford: Oxford University Press, 1986); and A. C. McGiffert, *A History of Christian Thought*, Vol. 2: *The West from Tertullian to Erasmus* (New York: Charles Scribner's Sons, 1933).

[25] Ian Knox remarks that to immanentist educators, including his dissertation supervisor Lee, "Prayer . . . is an intensification of purpose to act humanly." *Above or Within?*, 151–52, 91.

Critics have sensed the problem of "faith" in a religious instruction for behavior modification. Michael Warren said in 1970:

> . . . we must . . . recognize that man's response to the call of grace can take countless forms. It is difficult to see how this response can be properly channeled into specific behaviors predetermined by teacher and/or students without the risk of self-deception all around . . . If we are not careful, we can give learners merely the illusion of response.[26]

Accounts of religion in social sciences have been subjected to a critique similar to the analysis of faith. Anthropology, sociology, and religious studies each include several significant methodologies. Functional analyses of religion compete with more subjective methods that recognize the inward dimensions of religiosity. Gregory Baum affirms, "Since behavior is external, it can be studied with methods similar to those used in the natural sciences. But to study what this behavior means to the actors calls for understanding or interpretation, an approach that has no equivalent in the natural sciences."[27] He comments on the efforts of sociological pioneer Max Weber to account for subjectivity.

> In his opposition to positivism, Max Weber called his scientific approach *verstehende Soziologie*. It is possible to interpret this *verstehen* simply as a work of human intelligence, yet it is also possible to see it as a work demanding empathy, the emotional effort to put oneself in the shoes of others.[28]

Just to look at the external behavior does not capture the essence of religion. Lee's limitation of faith to its functions is not the only option. Operationalization simplifies faith to its visible results. The nature of good works is more complex than Lee credits. Any full account must include motivation, the factor which has to be inferred, as it is often unseen, and at times is unverifiable. Lee's understandings of faith in relation to action must be criticized as one-sided. Religion is more than what is seen.

Yet another reason for Lee's deficient idea of faith is that "faith" never means specifically Christian faith. Lee's faith is that of social scientists. For any universal scientific theory, "faith" must be universal. Such a "faith" is essential for the macrotheory to apply to "Jewish . . . Shinto . . . or what-

---

[26] Warren, "All Contributions," 29.
[27] Baum, "Remarks of a Theologian," 7.
[28] Baum, "Remarks of a Theologian," 7; cf. "The Impact of Sociology on Catholic Theology," 137.

ever."²⁹ Thus, faith is abstracted from its contents for purposes of analysis. Yet Christian faith is faith-in. Christian faith is trust in a specific historical person, that is, Jesus of Nazareth. Whether an idea of faith can be analyzed apart from the object of faith was a question of some who debated James Fowler's faith development proposals. Fowler proposed a universal theory of faith development, valid across cultures, and thus amenable to empirical measurements. Essayists in the volume of reaction doubted that Fowler referred to any particular faith.³⁰ Similarly, Lee expounds faith in general but the use of his theory with any particular faith is not a certainty.

Craig Gay notes a fashion of replacing theological terms with social science ones, asking whether the new terms are truly an advance. He wants to know if faith can be operationalized without omitting something. "Can it . . . be stated in social scientific language without loss?" He answers his question: social science restates what we already know in "currently-plausible language" but with a "costly revelance." He argues that the social sciences implicitly overlook a God-ward dimension; in a church context the result may be hollowed-out church practices.³¹ A theory of religious instruction appears to depend on its definition of faith. The issue is the definition of a faithful work. What is a work or act that God approves? The effort to operationalize faith, to assess it only by its visible, empirically verifiable results leads to a flattening of faith. Faith is not only action but must include motivation. A person could reproduce the outward form, that is, perform the behaviors, but lack the inner motivating power that is termed faith. The Jesus of the gospels indicted the religious leadership of his time for religious acts lacking right motivation.³² Superficial behavior is not true religion.

Dietrich Bonhoeffer offers an alternative construction of faith. Bonhoeffer was the German Lutheran pastor and theologian, imprisoned and martyred in 1945 by the Nazi government. Bonhoeffer produced a paradoxical definition of the faithful person in his widely appreciated *The*

---

[29] Lee, *Content*, 42, cited above pp. 34–35 [x-ref].

[30] E.g. Harry Fernhout, "Where is Faith?" in *Faith Development and Fowler*, eds. Craig Dykstra and Sharon Parks (Birmingham, Ala: Religious Education Press, 1986), 71–87.

[31] Craig Gay, "Evangelicals and the Language of Technopoly," *Crux*, 31 (1995) 32–40.

[32] Matthew 23 exposes formal religious acts done without proper motivation, picking up a theme also at Mark 7:6. See *Theological Dictionary of the New Testament* s.v. *présbys,* eds.G. Kittel and G. Friedrich, trans. G. Bromiley (Grand Rapids: Eerdmans, 1985). The prophets similarly criticized semblances of religious action; Hosea and Isaiah, among others, render devastating critiques of cult performances lacking religious motivation. The theme is frequent in the New Testament (e.g., Acts 5, 8, James 1:7, 2:2,15).

Cost of Discipleship: "Only those who believe obey; at the same time only those who obey believe."[33] His exposition is best read in its entirety, but a short version follows. Separating obedience from faith is a mistake. If we say that obedience "follows" faith chronologically, the question arises: when must obedience begin (69)? The answer has to be "immediately." Faith and obedience are not divorced in New Testament accounts such as Luke 9:57-62 (57). We must instead "place the one proposition that only he who believes is obedient alongside the other . . . "(69). "If we are to believe, we must obey a concrete command." Yet "we must add at once that this step is, and can never be more than, a purely external act and a dead work of the law . . . of course the work has to be done, but of itself it can never deliver from "bondage . . . " (71). Bonhoeffer is significantly and famously dealing with the danger of "cheap grace." He is speaking to a German Lutheran church in the 1930s that generally failed to match baptismal commitments with faithful acts. The affirmation of justification by faith seemed to lead to a faith seemed that was in words only. So "cheap grace" is grace taken for granted, the person failing in complementary actions (45).

Bonhoeffer's exposition stresses the human action side of the paradox. To provide a complement to Lee, one would need to underline the divine side of the formula. Bonhoeffer says in regard to the need for counterbalancing affirmations, "The Lutheran confessions . . . [h]aving effectively dealt with the danger of Pelagianism . . . find it both possible and necessary to leave room for the first external act which is the essential preliminary to faith" (70). There are two sides to faith, the human and the divine. In my opinion, Bonhoeffer's account has significant educational implications (74). However, because Lee has reduced faith to activity, the inwardness of faith is overlooked. His reduction of faith is consistent with his telescoping of transcendence into immanence.

A particular account of faith, a theology of faith, is essential to and inherent in Lee's theory of instruction. Supporting my argument, I conclude that Lee's functional "faith" is necessary to his theory, but is not necessarily enough for every educator.

Lee's Theology of Revelation

Like Lee's theology of faith, his theology of revelation underpins his social science religious instruction. Two themes are developed further here than

---

[33] Dietrich Bonhoeffer, *The Cost of Discipleship*, trans. R. H. Fuller (New York: Macmillan, [1937] 1963) 61–86, esp. 69.

in Chapter 2. First, Lee's revelation is an ongoing process. Revelation occurs within a human subject; revelation in scripture is granted incidental value only. Second, Lee's revelation is not primarily cognitive. The two themes combine to support Lee's progressive religious instruction. In the discussion of the themes I point to alternate conceptualizations. Like his view of faith, Lee's theology of revelation is not the only option for educators.

Revelation is Process

Revelation is generally considered as a supernatural phenomenon. By usual definition, revelation is data that is not immanent, not discoverable by natural means. Divine action is required to *reveal* the data. Thus, revelation could be a problem for a religious instruction that draws from immanent, discoverable, social-scientific sources only. Why is revelation not a problem to Lee?

The answer is that Lee's revelation is immanent. His revelation is akin to a process of scientific discovery. Revelation may be dramatic or it may be relatively tame but it is ongoing within the individual.[34] Lee says,

> The kerygma is basically a process, the process of Christification, of the flowing of Jesus into the teaching act and into the lives of both learner and teacher in a continuing ongoing revelation which is educative and salvific. Kerygma is, above all, a process approach to, and a process outcome of, the enterprise of religious instruction.[35]

This salvific education process may be set up

> not by telling the individual that such-and-such is God's word and he must be faithful to it, but instead by so structuring the learning situation whereby the individual is enabled to be faithful to his own experiencing. Once this happens, then the God flowing freely within the individual will be enabled as fully as possible to encounter the person at a deeply intersubjective level, that is the Person of God meeting at a point of contact with the human person. It is

---

[34] Lee, "Religious Instruction and Religious Experience," in *Handbook of Religious Experience*, ed. Ralph W. Hood (Birmingham, Ala: Religious Education Press, 1995), 537. " . . . religious experience is conceptualized as taking place at any and every level ranging from the delicate intimation of the transcendent awared upon seeing the sunlight glint of a wildflower in a May Alpine meadow to the most profound and intense of mystical experiences such as mystical marriage."

[35] Lee, *Shape*, 34.

then that religious instruction will have pedagogically created the conditions for pervasive, meaningful, and true fidelity to the ongoing revelation of God.[36]

Revelation in Lee's usage includes conversion and the action of the Holy Spirit. These inclusions are clear when Lee says above, "the God flowing freely within the individual will be enabled . . . to encounter the person at a deeply intersubjective level . . . the Person of God meeting . . . the human person." Revelation is nowhere objective. Lee omits a significant place for scripture, other than as source of proof texts. As revelation, scripture is subordinate to experience.[37] Scripture is the record of experiences with God.[38] The canon is less a history than a logbook of experiences. Lee's revelation is mainly or solely a process.

Revelation is Non-Cognitive

Second, Lee believes a truth encounter with God is mystical or ineffable. Words never do justice to reality. [39] He wages ongoing war against theology as a main expression of religion.[40] He can acknowledge that religion includes cognitive, affective and behavioral or lifestyle aspects, but "theology is simply a cognitive reflection upon religion, rather than religion itself."[41] Lee consistently minimizes the cognitive component of faith. " . . . [T]heology is fundamentally areligious in nature because as a cognitive science it does not intrinsically necessitate lifestyle religious practice on the part of the person engaging in scientific inquiry of a theological nature."[42] Again, "Revelation is not primarily or even essentially theology . . . Theology is just one way of cognitively reflecting on the nature and meaning of the [B]ible."[43]

---

[36] Lee, *Shape*, 37.

[37] Lee, *Shape*, 15.

[38] Lee "Religious Instruction and Religious Experience," 537. "Religious Education and the Bible: A Religious Educationist's View" includes a section entitled "The Bible is Essentially a Disclosure of Religious Experiences," 8–11. In *Biblical Themes in Religious Education*, ed. Joseph S. Marino (Birmingham, Ala: Religious Education Press, 1983).

[39] Lee, "Religious Instruction," 536–37. *Shape* lifts up Paul Tillich's detection of the priority of mystical encounters to a theological expression, 204.

[40] Lee, *Flow*, 15.

[41] Lee, *Content*, 39; "Authentic Source," 164.

[42] Lee, "CCD Renewal," 222; also "Vision, Prophecy and Forging the Future," 256.

[43] Lee, "Authentic Source," 133, also 100–110, 125.

This way of understanding revelation bears a significant implication for Lee's theory: Cognitive or linguistic accounts of reality are never the reality itself. Theory is theory and practice is practice. Therefore, empirical observation is able to supply an account of practice that theory never can.

> [T]he theology of practice is fundamentally different from practice itself, in this case from the practice of religious instruction . . . Theology does not provide a description of the intrinsic nature and workings of the particular reality itself. Thus the theology of a given reality is always a description external to a description of the reality in and of itself.[44]

Rephrasing elsewhere, Lee says, "There is a vast ontic difference between the theology of ecclesial practice and the practice itself. Theology is one kind of cognitive reflection on ecclesial practice; theology is not coextensive with ecclesial practice."[45] "It is not that the theology has been bad; rather it is that theology has been asked to do too much."[46]

With the above elements in place, the accompanying affirmation will seem natural. " . . . Social science is another way of listening to God and understanding his revelation."[47] With this affirmation, the transcendent God would seem to have moved entirely to the immanent. Experience is what really counts in education. Most dramatically, direct experience of God "break[s] open the crust that often encases religious substantive content so that we can behold face-to-face what is really fundamental and important in Christian living."[48] Contrariwise, " . . . [T]heology is not meant to be empirical."[49] Perhaps the clearest conjunction of Lee's social science empiricism with the priority of direct, or mystical, experience of God is on the last page of what may be the last volume of his published work:

---

[44] Lee, "Religious Instruction," 542–43

[45] Lee, "Authentic Source," 125; also see *Content*, 7, 40.

[46] Lee, *Flow*, 295.

[47] Lee, *Flow*, 295. An earlier hint is in *Shape*, 230–31, where Lee said "The new and still evolving concept of revelation makes it more possible for contemporary theologians to accept the social-science approach to religious instruction . . . Protestant and Catholic theologians are more and more pointing to revelation as a continuing process, rather than as a corpus of truths left as a deposit by the scriptures or by the historical Jesus."

[48] Lee, *The Sacrament Of Teaching: A Social Science Approach* (Birmingham, Ala.: Religious Education Press, 1999) 52; "Vision, Prophecy and Forging the Future," 257.

[49] Lee, *Shape*, 206.

> To concentrate on the religious instruction act is to listen attentively to its inner dynamisms with profound respect and humility, much as we listen to the rushing flow of a river or to the mighty sweep of the heaving ocean in order to authentically understand each and to harvest their power . . . We must listen to the act on its own terms, to its inner empirical dynamics, and not be clouded over by any a priori preconceptions or ideological orientations.[50]

Lee is not just against theology, he is against words. "We must listen to the act." Words are not adequate to convey experience. While such a stand might negate all instruction *per se*, Lee combines the aversion to cognition with empiricism and so avoids a potential negation. Empiricism gets beyond cognition. Lee accents the experience of the student over against what has traditionally been called "content." Lee wants students to "get it" but the "it" is ineffable. Names are labels we attach to experience. Theology thought itself to be tracing the parameters of the "it"—the experience of God. But words cannot convey the real; reality is unknowable. Words do not suffice. Reality is unspeakable. Direct experience is indispensable. To Lee, religious instruction's reliance on theology, intrinsically word-centered and cognitive, has been its downfall.[51] Theology cannot translate into practice.[52] Verbal revelation will not make a life change. Lee's nominalist, subjectivist epistemology is apparent.

Ironically, the readiness to have the empirical fact speak on its own terms means that its embedded ideological orientations pass unchallenged. Empirical fact is never bare or brute fact, as the previous chapter showed. Witnesses bring subjectivities. But an uncritical acceptance of fact means that no filter is in place to check systematic distortion. Lee implies that theology is a source of "ideological orientations"—but is ideology ever avoidable? The answer is No.

The embeddedness of theory with "fact" is not universally recognized in social science faculties. Mary Stewart Van Leeuwen detected two camps in the American Psychological Association, for instance, one camp scien-

---

[50] Lee, "Vision, Prophecy and Forging the Future," 266. *Flow* had a similar metaphor. "To use the social-science approach . . . is to be more true to God, since it is more in accord and harmony with the natural rhythm of the facilitation of learning in which the power of God flows as initiation, enablement, fruition, and completion," 295. Immanentism is on *Flow*'s surface at this point.

[51] For example, Lee, *Content*, 297.

[52] Lee, *Flow*, 270; "Authentic Source," 125, 164; *Content*, 7; "Vision, Prophecy and Forging the Future," 256, 263–64; "CCD Renewal," 222.

tistic, the other camp more hermeneutically attuned.[53] Facts are not as factual as we used to think. Lee will take all facts without discernment, it seems. The distorting effect of sin on perception is not addressed. Lee barely mentions that the world is askew. Empirical fact as such is good. Lee has no means to select good theory from bad. A Christian theory of instruction, on the other hand, must deal with the pervading reality of sin. Data is shaped by ideology and by the human tendency to label sin as something benign. Human beings actively resist truth—but Lee does not recognize any resistance.

Since Lee discounts both sin and the possibility of God's direct action, it is not surprising that conversion has little place either. The omission of conversion could be partly a "Catholic thing." Catholicism has what Thomas Groome has termed a humanitas anthropology,[54] meaning a generosity toward human nature in contrast to Protestant "pessimism." The sacrament of infant baptism is seen as partially effective for restoring human nature. On the other hand, some Catholic circles in recent decades have been paying significant attention to adult conversion. The restoration of the catechumenate and the adoption of a rite for adult initiates into the church are part of the renewed focus. Lee advocates a "red-hot religion" that he says can be taught,[55] but the necessity of a radical conversion or its character is not directly addressed in his writings, as far as I am aware. Lee characteristically says, "[R]eligious instruction stresses the process whereby the student can be most fruitfully taught to become a worthy son of God."[56] "Revelation" has some of the force of "conversion" for Lee. For him, the instructional process produces "revelation."

In the same way he overlooks conversion, Lee overlooks the direct activity of the Holy Spirit for making revelation come home to the learner. For Lee, God is wholly immanent and the Holy Spirit is inherent in the process, working through the process of instruction. As he presents it, this spiritual movement is not miraculous but wholly natural, one which any human being may experience at any time. No wonder the work of religious instruction represents an urgent apostolate. There could be no more religious work in the world—yet, ironically, at the same time, no less

---

[53] Her survey results are in "Psychology's 'Two Cultures': A Christian Analysis," *Christian Scholar's Review* 17 (1988) 406–24. She suggests the camps are inclined to positivism or to an interpretive stance by the dictates of their professional locations, extremes being experimentalists versus counselors.

[54] Thomas H. Groome, *Educating for Life* (Allen, Tex.: Thomas More, 1998) 195.

[55] Lee, "Vision, Prophecy and Forging the Future," 257.

[56] Lee, "The Teaching of Religion," 56–7.

religious work. Nature is all grace, so grace is only nature. Let it be said again: another construction is possible. Lee's assumption is not inevitable, and neither is the theory which builds on the assumption.

Other educators have the option of breaking apart the term "revelation." Lee's "revelation" covers theological ground that in other accounts would be more fully occupied by loci like conversion, the work of the Spirit, and an inscripturated, objective, revelation. Placing limits on the range of "revelation" allows space for theological elements as identified above. The effect of restoring the space of these loci would be to restore transcendence. Lee's "revelation" covers the semantic area it does because of his stress on immanence and empiricism requires the whole territory.

Religious Instruction Processes Revelation

Lee is proud to teach that process is itself a content. "Why is it that for so many centuries Catholic religious educators have incorrectly posited a fundamental separation between what they typically have termed "content" and "method," or more precisely between product content and instructional practice?" he asks. He says that the reason is the dominance of the "theological" model of religious instruction. As we are seeing, though, the contrast is not really to any non-theological model but to one based on an alternate theology. The basis for process as itself part of instructional content is Lee's idea of revelation. Process is the "religious" or pious content.

Lee says, for instance, "old and new testaments show quite clearly that in educating religious life in his people, God typically placed the learner(s) in an experiential situation." It might be objected that the revealed words themselves had value to the receiving community. After all, the words were preserved as scripture. Lee deals with this objection. "When verbal or intellectual elements were included, the scriptures clearly show that they were imbedded (sic) in a more generalized concrete experiential situation."[57] Thus he sees the process as more important than the content even in scripture.

Lee says the root of educational ineffectiveness is educators' failure to grasp learning as process. "There seems to be a strong, inbuilt denigration . . . of process-as-content . . . The first [reason] is the still prevalent conception . . . that revelation is a product content rather than a process content . . . revelation is regarded solely as a fixed, stable, unalterable body

---

[57] Lee, *Shape*, 15.

of product truths. . . ."⁵⁸ "[D]octrine . . . must be taught in such a way that it is inserted into the learner's experience."⁵⁹ Thus, the "task of the religion class is to so structure and recast the learner's experience that God's ongoing revelation is consciously, meaningfully, and affectively incorporated into the person's self-system and behavioral patterns of action.⁶⁰ In this statement, notice how a theological conception is clearly linked with an educational implication. The process is to grow out of Lee's theological insight. Simply said, not every educator need agree.

Lee's Immanent Divine Way

Immanentism is inherent in Lee's theory: " . . . nature is nature . . . because of the presence, power, and being of God . . . Wherever teaching and learning take place, God is intimately and existentially present in every zone of the process. Nature is . . . graced nature . . . "⁶¹

Once again, immanentism is not the only choice for understanding God's activity in the world. Ian Knox named three options in his *Above or Within?* (1976): "Supernatural Above the Natural," "Supernatural within the Natural," (Knox includes Lee), and supernatural and natural in "Equilibrium."⁶²

In North American religious education, immanence set against transcendence has prompted controversy since Horace Bushnell's *Christian Nurture* (1861). Sheldon Smith's 1941 volley against liberal Christian education includes six pages critiquing divine immanence, a main theme of American liberalism, along with the goodness of man, growth, and a re-imagined Jesus. Smith objects to "the idea of the God as the indwelling reality of the one organic and developing world-process" that is "implicit in [Bushnell's] doctrine of Christian nurture."

Perhaps one way of getting at Lee's issue is to ask whether absolute immanentism is essential to social science religious instruction. Lee himself recognized that it might be. "The supernatural element in religious

---

⁵⁸ Lee, *Content*, 89.

⁵⁹ Lee, *Shape*, 18.

⁶⁰ Lee, *Shape*, 16.

⁶¹ Lee, *Flow*, 292–3, op. cit., also *Shape*, 289.

⁶² Knox, *Above or Within?*, vii. In Catholic usage, supernatural does not necessarily mean miraculous but "whatever transcends nature; whatever cannot be included in the reality of the purely natural." See Stanley J. Grenz and Roger E. Olsen, *20th Century Theology: God and the World in a Transitional Age* (Downers Grove, Ill: InterVarsity, 1992) 244–45. Grenz and Olsen use the theme of immanence in tension with transcendence to organize the varying accents of theologians.

instruction introduces a new and strong variable which . . . would seem to place a difficult if not insuperable obstacle in the path of . . . operationalizing the objectives of religious instruction. . . ."[63]

Stating the question in another way, would Lee's religious instruction stand on a purist transcendist foundation? Could a thoroughgoing transcendist adopt the social science religious instruction macrotheory?[64]

However, such ways of framing the question fall into an either-or trap. It is not either immanence or transcendence, but Knox's third alternative, that likely includes most educators. Knox's conclusion desires "equilibrium," that both transcendence and immanence to be expressed in religious education.[65] In line with Lee's admission above, let us grant that a pure transcendist, if one could be found, would not endorse social science religious instruction. But see: Lee performs a labeling exercise. He set up all opponents as transcendists. Certainly he is able to recognize that a spectrum of opinion could exist. He says that when pushed to choose, his choice is immanence over transcendence.[66] But he clusters his rivals on the opposite pole. He produces profiles that press the reader to perceive that all other educators must require out-of-the-sky divine education.[67]

By contrast, here is an historical anomaly. Sheldon Smith's neo-orthodox theology leans toward transcendence. Smith doubts Bushnell's system but he grants that Bushnell "opened a way to mitigate some of the cruder forms of supernaturalism." He grants that Bushnell saw the contemporary trend to naturalism and wished to make space for "the activity of the supernatural in [his] unified system."[68] Smith's approval of a mitigation of supernaturalism seems significant. It shows that non-immanentists like Smith are not necessarily one-sided.

Another anomaly: the "transcendist" *Lumen Vitae* theorists of Lee's generation. These transcendists used psychological studies in their catechesis. Writers including Marcel van Caster did not proscribe immanent

---

[63] Lee, *Shape*, 70.
[64] Ian Knox thought that social science religious instruction could work on a transcendist foundation. Above, Chapter 1, 28–29, n. 69 [x-ref].
[65] Knox, *Above or Within?*, 157–60.
[66] Lee, "Prediction in Religious Education," 43: "it is the immanent which is of crucial importance," *Shape*, 208, 272–81.
[67] Lee, "Authentic Source," 133–34; *Flow*, 174–80, also 42, 148, 165, 185, 203–204.
[68] Sheldon Smith, *Faith and Nurture* (New York: Scribner's, 1941) 5–10; Randolph Crump Miller has comments in "Theology in the Background," in *Religious Education and Theology*, ed. Norma H. Thompson (Birmingham, Ala: Religious Education Press, 1982) 18.

empirical data.[69] How is it possible? The situation invites further investigation. Lee has painted the supposed transcendists with too broad a brush.

The real question is not whether transcendists might adopt Lee's theory. The real question is whether non-immanentists must recognize the macrotheory as inevitable. Are all educators, immanentist and transcendist and "equilibrist," required to adopt social science religious instruction?

At one extreme, educators of a purely transcendist position clearly will not rule out theology's role in educational methodology. Revelation in one-sided fashion as objective or literal will dictate methodology. This is the divine action extreme of the spectrum. If we were to imagine a conference of transcendists, Lee would fail to convince them because he assumes that modern immanentist theology is the only kind that will stand scrutiny.

Knox's "equilibrium" alternative is that God's transcendence and immanence are viewed as both-and propositions, not either-or ones.[70] God is both transcendent and immanent. God is above the creation, distinct, but also active within it. For scriptural support it would be enough to compare Isaiah 40 with Acts 17 or Philippians 2:12, 13. God's transcendence and immanence both receive generous canonical expression. The tension between the affirmations is left unresolved. Both lines of thinking are true simultaneously.

Moving beyond the Biblical lack of resolution is a gigantic theological task. Knox says that while both "polar emphases" are true, it is "difficult to live with the tension that comes from a *full* assertion of transcendence and immanence . . . we tend to favor one or the other."[71] The observation is true on the personal level. Beyond a personal analysis, entire theological systems and their historical institutional expressions hinge in part on the community's view of Christ in relation to human culture—immanent, transcendent, paradoxical, or transformist. H. Richard Niebuhr's classic typology labeled five historical-cultural-theological paradigms encompassing most if not all Christian expressions. Varying attitudes towards God's immanence and transcendence figure prominently in Niebuhr's analysis of the paradigms.

Niebuhr's typology of expressions of Christian faith, though it has encountered criticism, still serves many scholars as a rough and ready

---

[69] Boys, *Educating in Faith*, 96–7.

[70] For example, Knox, *Above or Within?*, 156.

[71] Knox, *Above or Within?*, 156.

guide to theological location.⁷² The typology shows how culture, history, and theological commitments interact for a community expression. We can use Niebuhr's analysis even if we acknowledge that its categories are somewhat forced, or that it is set up to favor Niebuhr's fifth, final category, or that the approach tends to relativize revelation.

In the typology, Lee would fit as a Christ-of-culture Christian. He recounts his conversion from "ultraconservative religiosity" to an "espousal of a progressive liberal religious stance," which change "enabled me to see realities and embrace positions which my previous restrictive reactionary religious worldview would have prevented."⁷³ Here is more than a passing resemblance to the experience of liberal educator George Coe, who once judged that "the most significant turning point in my life, religiously considered, was this early turning away from dogmatic method to scientific method."⁷⁴ Lee in his first decade of teaching could write,

> . . . when Catholic schoolmen were less sophisticated and more ghettoistic than they are in today's open Church, the epithet "those godless public schools" was hurled with great frequency. . . . Nothing in God's world is godless. Indeed, public schools . . . do provide a Catholic education in the sense that the outcomes derived from these schools lead the student to God.⁷⁵

This is not a transformist stance, where Christ is seen as able to adapt, influence, and transform culture; rather it is one in which Christ is already inherent in culture. Quotes could be multiplied for earlier and later years.⁷⁶ Those who share Lee's theological stance will endorse his educa-

---

⁷² Niebuhr, *Christ and Culture*. Criticism may be reviewed in the volume *Authentic Transformation*, eds. Glen Stassen et. al. (Nashville: Abingdon, 1996), especially the essay by J. H. Yoder.

⁷³ Lee, "To Basically Change Fundamental Theory and Practice,", in *Modern Masters of Religious Education*, ed. Marlene Mayr (Birmingham, Ala: Religious Education Press, 1983) 281.

⁷⁴ Quoted in Boys, *Educating in Faith*, 50.

⁷⁵ Lee, *The Purpose of Catholic Schooling* (Washington, DC, and Dayton, Ohio: National Catholic Education Association, and Pflaum, 1968) 11.

⁷⁶ For example, Lee, *Principles and Methods of Secondary Education*, (New York: McGraw-Hill, 1963): "No knowledge, therefore, can be completely secular; all knowledge is God-soaked . . . Original sin is important in that it created a disjointedness (but not a separation) between natural and supernatural; however, the fact of the Redemption with its healing effect must never be forgotten." Note how theological underpinnings in Lee's theorizing are bare in the quote. Also *Flow*, 178; "Authentic Source," 124: "a world that God created and suffuses."

tion, in general at least.[77] But religious educators do not fit the Christ-of-culture type uniformly. Many are likely paradoxists or transformists or advocates of Christ against culture. Their ways of using empirical findings in education will be influenced by the accent on transcendence of those theological stances.

Since it lacks adequate recognition of God's transcendence, Lee's immanentism could tend to pantheism or panentheism. Lee said, "... nature, teacing, learning, and man are not separated in any way over against God ... Nature ... is graced nature." Pantheism is the identification of God and the world as one and the same; the distinction between Creator and creation is ignored or denied. Panentheism makes God greater than the creation, and the creation an overflow of his power and presence. While few Christians would adopt either position without significant qualification, pantheism or panentheism are labels that follow Rahner or Teilhard.[78] Lee quotes Teilhard in a number of places, as noted, and Rahner less frequently. It would be a mistake to over-label Lee as pantheist or panentheist. It is appropriate, though, to point out an exposure that arises from one-sided immanentism.

Again, the question for our purpose is whether all non-immanentist educators, a majority, must adopt the social science religious instruction macrotheory. The answer is No. Non-immanentist educators need not adopt the social science religious instruction macrotheory.

Conclusion

This survey of Lee's theology has not been exhaustive. I have shown that Lee's theory is not universal by showing foundational theological assertions. All implications need not be covered. Lee's implicit theology of church and society, for instance, is atomic and individualist; community or even family structures receive little attention. But this observation is not essential to our purpose. Lee has not worked out a systematic theology; he

---

[77] Ian Knox profiles three "immanentist" educators and notes that they "propose apparently quite different approaches ... the *same* theological overview may correlate with *different* theoretical approaches to religious education." *Above or Within?*, 149. A historical-cultural-personal-theological matrix produces an educational expression. "... [T]heological metaperspective may be compared to the light filtering through tinted glass and suffusing the whole ... ", 149.

[78] See, for example, Grenz and Olsen, *Twentieth-Century Theology*, 253–54; J. J. Duyvené de Wit, "Pierre Teilhard de Chardin," in *Creative Minds in Contemporary Theology*, ed. Philip E. Hughes (Grand Rapids: Eerdmans, 1966) 438–48; Hendrikus Berkhof, *Two Hundred Years of Theology*, trans J. Vriend (Grand Rapids: Eerdmans, 1989) 235–36, 242–47.

is an educator. Yet more than once he returns to his basic positions on the nature of faith, on revelation, and on God as immanent. The reader has before him or her the theology essential to social science religious instruction.

The ability to specify theological components makes clear that Lee's theory is neither generic nor universal in scope. Those who propose a macrotheory must show that the theory is independent of a particular theology. Lee's commitments are not universal or inescapable for every theologically-committed educator. Lee has a definite theology to which all educators do not subscribe. Lee's theory is not neutral, nor, as claimed, able to serve as a "foundation" across differing theologies and religious claims. My exposure of Lee's theology undermines his claim that social science religious instruction is a macrotheory for religious education.

Lee's presuppositions carry their own distinct educational potentialities. An educator who posits a given starting point finds perspectives on social sciences and religious instruction that fit. Education proposals generally express prior commitments, and Lee's theory is also an expression of commitments. Lee serves educators as a case study in the interlocking nature of philosophical-theological commitments and a theory of education. His theory grows from its theological stance.

Chapter 4 looks at the significance of empiricism for religious education.

4
Conclusions

BERARD Marthaler, editor of the Catholic catechetical periodical *The Living Light*, wrote in 1976 that disciplinary status for religious education depends on the development of methodology.[1] In the years since his statement there have been new movements toward a foundation; liberation theology and narrative theology are two. Theological feminism and black theology, variants of liberation theology, offer significant corrections by challenging long-standing oversights. In some quarters, the critical realist philosophy of Thomas F. Torrance is teamed with hermeneutical theory such as that of Hans-Georg Gadamer toward a theory-consistent practice.[2] Among Catholics, dedicated laity and clergy continue to pursue the revival of the catechumenate in publications, on the Internet and through conventions. But consensus in the field seems no closer than in 1976. Marthaler's comment remains on target.

Emmanuel Levinas once wrote, "Those who have concerned themselves with method all their lives have written a lot of books in the place of the more interesting books which they did not write."[3] Methodology can be boring. But methodology is also as crucial as James Michael Lee sees it to be. As a young priest, Thomas Groome had a question for himself after successfully teaching religion to a class of adolescents: "What was I doing?" Groome inquired about the underpinnings of his already operative

---

[1] Berard L. Marthaler, "Discipline in Search of an Identity: Religious Education," *Horizons* 3 (1976) 205–9. Marthaler cites Lee in the article.

[2] James Loder's *The Logic of the Spirit* (San Francisco: Jossey-Bass, 1998) or *The Transforming Moment: Understanding Convictional Experiences* (San Francisco: Harper & Row, 1981) is an instance, as is his student Robert K. Martin's *The Incarnate Ground of Christian Faith: Toward a Christian Theological Epistemology for the Educational Ministry of the Church* (Lanham, MD: University Press of America, 1998).

[3] Culled from Jeffrey W. Robbins, "Replacing Theology," retrieved from <http://web.syr.edu/~jwrobbin/replace.html> on February 26, 2004.

method.⁴ Granted that theory is not sharply divided from practice, that practice itself brings insight, ⁵ methodology is a basis for continually improving practice. Because of the fragmentation of the religious education field, however, one more model is not a significant contribution in and of itself. Methodologies that lend confidence to practice, ruling out some approaches and throwing light on others, are the need of the day.

It must be said clearly: James Michael Lee saw a crying need for critical religious educational practice, and his contribution aimed to fill the gap. Lee says,

> I firmly believe that one major cause for the relative inefficacy of much of contemporary religious instruction lies in the fact that most religion teachers hold one theory of religious instruction while at the same time they utilize pedagogical practices drawn from another highly-conflicting theory. Consistency in the relationship between theory and practice is absolutely indispensable for the effectiveness, expansiveness, and fruitfulness of a practice.⁶

Harold Burgess and also Kevin Coughlin see these words as fundamental to Lee's project.⁷ Lee pursued consistent methodology. Educators do not have to buy into Lee's theory to agree that good methodology is crucial.

The Appreciation of Empirical Data

In later years, Lee called himself a prophet. The designation might have been his recognition that his cause would need time to come into its own. But Lee's prophetic stance is a protest too. Lee objects to the vagueness of religious education. He wanted a theory that would support empirical study. One could even say that Lee perceived numbers to be so valuable that he constructed a theory to support their consistent usage.

Quantification has good uses. In *What Works on Wall Street*, James O'Shaughnessy laments the way investors trust their instincts. The tendency makes them prey to personal preferences and emotion. "Investment

---

⁴ Groome tells the story in the first pages of his *Christian Religious Education: Sharing Our Story and Vision* (San Francisco: Harper, 1980).

⁵ Joseph Dunne, *Back to the Rough Ground: Practical Judgment and the Lure of Technique* (Notre Dame: University of Notre Dame Press, 1993) 268.

⁶ Lee, *Flow*, 27.

⁷ Harold Burgess, "Toward a Synapse of Theory and Practice," in *Modern Masters of Religious Education*, ed. Marlene Mayr (Birmingham, Ala: Religious Education Press, 1983); Kevin Coughlin, "Religious Education in Everyday Life," 129.

advice bombards us . . . with little to support it but anecdotal accounts. Many managers will give a handful of stocks as examples, demonstrating how well they went on to perform." Advisors "ignore the many other stocks that also possessed the preferred characteristics but failed. . . . There's often a chasm . . . between what we think might work and what really works." Quantification can challenge received or taken-for-granted wisdom. Empirical theologian Johannes Van der Ven similarly says that without empiricism, practical theology could be "only rough guesses."[8] Roderick Martin seconds Van der Ven: "[C]riticism based upon objective facts is obviously preferable to criticism based upon random anecdotes."[9] Of course, more must be said about the quality of "objective." But a nagging realism attaches to empirical quantification. Human beings are prone to self-deception.[10] Lee, for instance, demolishes theological pronouncements on the effects of isolation on seminarians with quantitative studies.[11] Like financial advisor O'Shaughnessy, theorists find empirical study to be a corrective.

An Overlooked Circle

Numbers can be overemphasized. Positivism continues to be the dominant mood of social and political science departments, Gregory Baum notes. Baum calls the commitment to positivism a mood rather than the result of reflection on foundational issues. "What often characterizes [sociologists] is the wish to assimilate the social sciences . . . to the natural sciences . . . [they] search for plausible hypotheses, continue . . . research to demonstrate these hypotheses, and . . . make predictions about human behavior."[12] The problem is the lack of critical reflection on the deterministic idea of humanness embedded in the procedure. The sociologist's philosophical or theological commitments are never brought into contact with the received methodology. The fault is not all that of sociology. Philosophy

---

[8] Johannes A. Van der Ven, *Practical Theology: An Empirical Approach* (Kampen: Kok Pharos, 1993) 20.

[9] Roderick Martin, "Sociology and Theology: Alienation and Original Sin," in *Theology and Sociology: A Reader*, ed. Robin Gill (London: Cassell, 1996) 115.

[10] A literature exists on the topic. For example, Eduardo Giannetti, *Lies We Live By: The Art of Self-Deception* (London: Bloomsbury, 2001); Alfred R. Mele, *Self-Deception Unmasked* (Princeton: Princeton University Press, 2001). The Worldcat multi-library database lists more than 200 titles in response to a subject search March 12, 2004 at <http://www.columbia.edu>.

[11] Lee, *Shape*, 194–95.

[12] Gregory Baum, "Sociology and Theology," 25.

departments, which could elucidate methodological questions, have been occupied in other directions. Paul Lazarsfeld, a premier empirical sociologist of an earlier generation at Columbia University, complained, "Philosophers of science are not interested in and do not know what a work-a-day empirical research man does. This has two consequences: either we have to become our own methodologists or we have to muddle along without benefit of the explicating clergy."[13] Baum implies that, unfortunately, Lazarsfeld's muddling-along option is as frequently taken as the other option.

Some capable and articulate sociologists and philosophers who do explicate methodology are "post-positivists." Among these are Paul Kincaid, and, in educational research, D. C. Phillips and Nicholas C. Burbules.[14] These theorists sense the mood of post-modernism and hear the critique of positivism. The challenge to apparent objectivity and the recovery of human subjectivity evidenced by the variety of "isms" are taken seriously. The post-positivists give recognition to non-empirical research but assert the unmatchable value of empirical research. "Hard" and "soft" researches are to co-exist as perspectives. However, what is missing in post-positivism is an accounting for researcher worldview. The post-positivists have not accounted for the tinted fact, so their dissent from positivism is only partial.

Perhaps the significant dissidents who explicate methodology are the critical theorists. Critical theory understands that ideology is imbued in "the facts." Mainly housed at the Institute for Social Research in Frankfurt, Germany, since the 1920s, its methodologists included Karl Mannheim, Ernst Troeltsch (a theologian), and Jürgen Habermas. Other names are Erich Fromm, Max Scheler, and Max Horkheimer, plus the naturalized American Herbert Marcuse, the Italian Antonio Gramsci, and Michel Foucault. Stephen Brookfield includes all within the "traditions of criticality."[15]

---

[13] Paul F. Lazarsfeld, "Philosophy of Science and Empirical Social Research," in *Logic, Methodology and the Philosophy of Science*, ed. Ernest Nagel, Patrick Suppes and Alfred Tarski (Stanford: Stanford University Press, 1962) 463–73, cited in Bryant, *Positivism in Social Theory and Research*, 144.

[14] Harold Kincaid, *Philosophical Foundations of the Social Sciences: Analyzing Controversies in Social Research* (Cambridge: Cambridge University Press, 1996); D. C. Phillips and Nicholas C. Burbules, *Postpositivism and Educational Research* (Lanham, Md.: Rowman and Littlefield, 2000).

[15] Stephen Brookfield, "Critical Theory and Adult Learning," unpublished manuscript, 6.

The Institute for Social Research conducted social research! It sometimes escapes notice that while critical theory is best known for ideological sociology, the Institute did engage in empirical study. "The most sophisticated of the Institute's researches gave rise to a series of publications on Authority and Family of almost a thousand pages, without even getting beyond the pilot stage." Bryant reports an assessment that the critical theorists "were the leading empirical social researchers in Weimar Germany, and [other] social researchers . . . were much less sophisticated. . . ."[16] The reminder of their empirical capability is important. Not necessarily does empirical research have to be pitted against qualitative research. "Hard" numbers-oriented studies do not cancel out "soft" studies. Neither do the researches have to remain unrelated perspectives. The sociologists who were and are most clearly ideological had a carefully elaborated empirical program. At the Frankfurt Institute the empirical research was expressly value laden. As Baum said, research is value-laden always.[17] Marcuse in the 1960s affirmed the possibility of empirical social science, and Fay has done so more recently.[18]

Researches outside the critical tradition are less obvious in parlaying a worldview but are no less tendentious. Among psychologists, for instance, Freudians have research with numbers; Skinnerians have research with numbers; Jungians have research with numbers. The numbers bid to confirm a worldview. The recognition is no more than Ellis Nelson said in his gentle refutation of Lee's *Flow*.[19] All theorists, not only Lee, inevitably bring a worldview to their number gathering. The inevitability is clear in the fact that similar "social scientific" studies produce such different results.[20]

Are all empirical studies somehow "true"? The philosopher of science Paul Feyerabend once wrote *Against Method* to suggest that progress in science happens by mistakes. "Science is an essentially anarchistic enterprise:

---

[16] Bryant, *Positivism in Social Theory and Research*, 118.

[17] Above, 62.

[18] Brookfield, "Building a Critical Theory of Adult Learning," Chapter 1, unpublished manuscript, citing B. Fay, *Critical Social Science: Liberation and its Limits* (Ithaca, N.Y.: Cornell University Press, 1987) xi. Brookfield notes that the validity of empirical confirmation is debated within "criticality," some theorists rejecting quantitative measure as "a misplaced application of positivist technical-rationality."

[19] Above, 46 [x-ref].

[20] Above, 63 [x-ref].

theoretical anarchism is . . . more likely to encourage progress than its law-and-order alternatives."[21] He was not taken entirely seriously.[22]

Gregory Baum can take a similar approach. He points out differences between Hegel, Marx and Toennies but claims, "There is no reason why these different theories could not all be true at the same time." This is because "[r]eligion is a highly complex, many-leveled, ambivalent phenomenon; and even if these theories offer mutually exclusive explanations, they may well refer to diverse layers and trends in religion, each with different characteristics and different social effects."[23] There is value in Baum's assessment, but caution should be sounded too.

On the positive side of Baum's assertion, religion is indeed multifaceted and complex, as complex as human life gets. The most basic issues of human living are joined in the area "religion." From depth of conviction comes religion's potential to generate deep disagreement. It may be a mistake to mark off religion as somehow separate and definable. Since worldview is religious, the whole of one's being is wrapped up in "religion." Religion is inescapable. "Religion is Life," as a Reformed festschrift once affirmed. Everyone is possessed by a religion, tenable or untenable.[24] Comparative religion may be as close as we can get to knowing ourselves. Analysis without the benefit of comparison is already and at once "within" one's worldview.

The challenging aspect of Baum's statement is in the caveat, "even if mutually exclusive." Baum's caveat hints at an ultimate unknowability of reality. Is Baum inviting readers to accept irrationality as the furthest that human intellect can penetrate? If so, while the approaches to social science empiricism are very different, Baum is approaching Lee's disavowal of words for representing reality. I return to the issue of multiple truths versus rationality below.

Empiricism depends on a prior philosophy or worldview. Worldview is deeper and more tenacious than a philosophy. James Olthuis describes it thus:

---

[21] Feyerabend, *Against Method: Outline of an Anarchistic Theory of Knowledge* (London: NLB, 1975) 10.

[22] Bryant remarks that no version of unity of scientific method has been agreed on, from Comte to Popper, and some philosophers of science 'dispute the idea of unity of method even in natural science, as Feyerabend, with his sorties *Against Method* vividly testifies." Bryant, *Positivism in Social Theory*, 6–7.

[23] Baum, *Religion and Alienation*, 85.

[24] James H. Olthuis, "On Worldviews," *Christian Scholar's Review* 14 (1985) 153–64.

> For each adherent, a worldview gives reasons and impetus for deciding what is true and what really matters in . . . experience. In other words, a worldview functions both *descriptively and normatively*. It has what Clifford Geertz calls a dual focus: it both tells us what is the case (and what is not the case) and tells us what ought (and ought not) to be the case. A worldview is both a sketch of and a blueprint for reality; it both describes *what we see and stipulates what we should see.*[25]

The comprehensiveness of worldview circles again to the way the scientist perceives:

> What counts as an "evidencing reason" for a belief in one context will be seen as evidence for quite a different conclusion in another context. For example, was the fact that living matter appeared in Pouchet's laboratory preparations evidence for the spontaneous generation of life, or evidence of the incompetence of the experimenter, as Pasteur maintained? As historians of science have shown, different scientists drew different conclusions and took the evidence to point in different directions. This was possible because *something is only evidence for something else when set in the context of assumptions which give it meaning*—assumptions, for instance, about what is probable or improbable.[26]

Similarly, culture, philosophy, location in history, or worldview predispose an observer toward some interpretations of fact, dispose him or her to overlook interpretations, and leads the investigator against some interpretations.

Murray Murphey completes the circle of human subjectivity. He summarizes research showing how the ideas of what constitutes empirical fact vary from culture to culture. Murphey recalls anthropologist Irving Hallowell's 1940s studies of the Ojibwa people, where Hallowell researched the Ojibwa sense of personhood. Hallowell found that "concepts of the self, time, space, the objects in the environment, the persons in the environment, and the norms for evaluating these were all culturally variable." The "difference in psychological structure between [the Ojibwa] and

---

[25] James H. Olthuis, "On Worldviews," emphasis mine. See also Elliott Eisner, *The Educational Imagination* (New York: Macmillan, 1979) 46: "Descriptive theory is in a subtle but important sense pervaded by normative theory. . . ."

[26] Barry Barnes and David Bloor, "Relativism, Rationalism and the Sociology of Knowledge," in *Science, Reason, and Reality: Issues in the Philosophy of Science*, ed. Daniel Rothbart (Fort Worth: Harcourt Brace, 1998) 328. Emphasis mine. Kuhn the historian of science includes many such instances.

contemporary Americans, Hallowell was able to explain in terms of the relationships the Ojibwa conceived to exist between themselves and other-than-human "persons" [who] inhabited their environment." Importantly for our purpose, "religion tended to be subsumed within the world view, where spirits became one of several classes of persons with whom the self interacted, and the "soul" became a particular way of conceptualizing the self."[27]

It is in an anthropological context that Robert Bellah can affirm religion. If religion is defined as "a set of symbolic forms and acts that relate man to the ultimate conditions of his existence," then "religion is a part of the species life of man, as central to his self-definition as speech." And,

> If we define religion as that symbol system that serves to evoke what Herbert Richardson calls the "felt-whole," that is, the totality that *includes subject and object* and provides the context in which life and action finally have meaning, then I am prepared to claim that as Durkheim said of society, religion is a reality *sui generis*. To put it bluntly, religion is true.[28]

Religion is true, that is, as an observable influencer of life or as "social fact." Bellah is not saying that "any particular religious proposition can claim to represent a truth that transcends the cultural and social realms."[29] He is recognizing religions as social facts, as worldviews that account for experience. Murphey sums up,

> [E]xperience is never pure; perception is inferential and conditioned by perceptual hypotheses that are part of the theoretical system. Thus which sorts of theories are empirical—that is, are supported by evidential experience—and which are not is a question answered from within each theoretical system separately.[30]

John Milbank affirms the insight: "sociology is inevitably at variance with the perspectives of many traditional religions, which make no sepa-

---

[27] Murray G. Murphey, "On the Scientific Study of Religion in the United States, 1870–1980," in *Religion and Twentieth-Century American Intellectual Life*, ed. Michael J. Lacey (Cambridge: Cambridge University Press, 1989) 149.

[28] Murphey, "Scientific Study of Religion," 159–61, quoting Robert Bellah, *Beyond Belief* (New York: Harper & Row, 1970) 21, 223, 252–53.

[29] Murphey, "Scientific Study of Religion," 161. Also Arthur L. Greil, "Meaning and Modernity: Religion, Polity, and Self" (Book Review), *Sociology of Religion*, (Summer 2003), retrieved from <http://www.findarticles.com> on Dec. 26, 2003.

[30] Murphey, "Scientific Study of Religion," 170.

ration between 'religious' and 'empirical' reality. . . ."[31] Pressing the same point home by shock, Murphey adds "No one who has read the writings of New England Puritans can doubt that doctrines such as innate depravity and predestination were for them thoroughly grounded in experience, and therefore empirical doctrines. . . ."[32] The system produces the facts. "If Calvinism is to be rejected, it is because we regard some alternative view of the world as offering a better account of experience, not because there was anything inherently untestable or unempirical about Calvin's theory."[33] To argue "facts" is, at least in part, to argue a worldview also.[34]

Lee founds his theory of religious instruction on a distinction between religious and empirical. Rather than establishing a universally-valid theory, Lee repeats a construction of Western culture.

Our consideration of Lee's theory has brought us to this summary: Lee affirms empirical immnent data against others who put stock only in revealed data. For educational methodology, he sets empirically validated results against all theology. To Lee, theology only makes the water muddy. Theology detracts from clarity. Lee forces a choice between immanent and transcendent data: Either human or divine sources must direct our religious educational task. We have seen, however, that Lee fails to reckon that social scientific data has a metaphysics already. Yet recognizing observer subjectivity does not solve the problem of an epistemology for religious instruction. Observer subjectivity introduces irrationalism. North American social science until the 1960s was surely empiricist. It tended to reduce religion (and other aspects of human living) to religion's functions.

However, accepting the presence of worldviews within empirical data brings no criteria to choose among the worldviews. As Walter Wyman observes, "Every worldview is conditioned historically and therefore limited and relative. *A frightful anarchy of thought appears.*"[35] Either pre-sixties empiricism or post-sixties irrationalism must rule, it appears.

---

[31] Milbank, *Theology and Social Theory*, 106.

[32] Murphey, "Scientific Study of Religion," 170.

[33] Ibid., 169.

[34] Mark Noll, "Traditional Christianity and the Possibility of Historical Knowledge," *Christian Scholar's Review* 19 (1990) 388–406.

[35] Walter E. Jr. Wyman, Jr, "The Historical Consciousness and the Study of Theology," in *Shifting Boundaries: Contextual Approaches to the Structure of Theological Education*, ed. Barbara G. Wheeler and Edward Farley (Louisville: Westminster John Knox, 1991) 98, quoting Sarah Coakley, "Theology and Cultural Relativism: What Is the Problem?" *Neue Zeitschrift für Systematische Theologie und Religion* 21 (1979) 223–43, emphasis mine.

Baum's solution to irrationalism is that educators choose researchers whose subjectivities are similar to their own. Since research always bears values, educators are deliberately to choose research done in a congruent perspective. This is valuable advice. It is definitely preferable to naïve use of social scientific data. But the field of religious education will not be more unified by this recognition alone. It will become less unified if the recommendation is an isolated recommendation. Religious education will merely express the subjectivities of the many individuals who contribute theory. Without a way to bridge objective and subjective, the result of Baum's recognition is irrationalism and, finally, anti-intellectualism.

Baum's solution tends to solipsism. The *Oxford English Dictionary* defines solipsism as the view or theory that self is the only object of real knowledge or the only thing really existent.[36] Objective reality is unknowable, since subjects only know their own experience. The world is subjective. The *Cambridge Dictionary of Philosophy* expands the definition by distinguishing varieties of solipsism. For us, the most relevant definition of solipsism is the view that human subjects are isolated from other sentient beings because we can never adequately understand their experience, or again, that meanings or referents of all words are mental entities accessible only to the language user. Baum expands solipsism by making knowledge a community activity.[37] Like-minded persons should confer.[38] But worldviews are incommensurable. Translation, dialogue, or correlation are apparently not options. Kuhn was criticized for exactly this issue, for having introduced radical relativism to "hard" science. Kuhn said in effect that one paradigm is as good as another,[39] that as far as we can know, Ptolemy is as true to reality as Copernicus. Feyerabend's anarchist proposal merely af-

---

[36] *Oxford English Dictionary* s.v. "solipsism," retrieved from <http://www.columbia.edu> on Mar. 2, 2004.

[37] Social solipsism is possible. Kuhn names it and calls it parochialism, 193.

[38] *Cambridge Dictionary of Philosophy*, s.v. 'solipsism'. Exploration of this area is beyond the scope of this dissertation. George Lindbeck's *The Nature of Doctrine*, for instance, puts forward a community-based epistemology as a way beyond the confines of "propositional" and "experiential-expressive" systems. Lindbeck's proposal is "cultural-linguistic." Lindbeck matches implicit nominalism with agnosticism about reality. Lindbeck, *The Nature of Doctrine: Religion and Theology in a Postliberal Age* (Philadelphia: Fortress Press, 1983). However, Jeff Astley and others include a selection from Lindbeck's book in their *Theological Perspectives of Christian Formation* (Grand Rapids: Eerdmans, 1996) and so indirectly affirm that the most basic theological considerations feed directly into religious education theory.

[39] Kuhn attempts to deal with the objection in his postscript to the 1970 edition. Kuhn, 206.

firms Kuhn's relativist stream of thought. But with anarchy no principle of choice is available. To affirm anarchy in method is to affirm that reality is irrational. "It" is mystical or unknowable. Words never penetrate reality's shell and are arbitrary labels only.

On one hand, empirical science has made a marked contribution. The contribution has been possible because the world and human culture are measurable and thus scientific progress is possible. A world is really out there to be known. Karl Mannheim, the critical theorist, recognizes this:

> . . . positivism did commit itself to onto logical judgments, despite its anti-metaphysical prejudices. . . . Its faith in progress and its naïve realism in specific cases are examples. . . . It was precisely those presuppositions which enabled *positivism to make so many significant contributions.*[40]

On the other hand, Kuhn and others oblige us to recognize that the mind and culture shape all knowledge. All truth is not God's truth, not in any straightforward way.

Would-be knowers therefore find themselves on the horns of a dilemma. Either reason can give us the world (but subject is absent), or reason can give us an actively ordering observer (no sure object).[41] The dilemma appears, for instance, in a passage of Don Browning's. Browning recognizes that modern psychologies serve to legitimate economic structures of society.[42] This is the subjective side of knowledge; Browning accepts that interest shapes knowledge.[43] But on the other hand, Browning does not wish to discard what he sees as modern psychology's valuable insights. The objective side of knowledge, a realism, intrudes. Logically, Browning's recognition of the subjective side should cause him to abandon modern psychology; its authority is so variable. But advances have been made! The objective advance appears undeniable and the realization brings hesitation. Subjective and objective have not been reconciled.

The history of thought shows oscillation between subjective and objective. The shift of emphasis goes back to philosophy's dawn. In this area Reformed epistemologists who follow Cornelius Van Til offer valu-

---

[40] Karl Mannheim, "Theology and the Sociology of Knowledge," in *Theology and Sociology: A Reader,* enlarged ed., ed. Robin Gill (London: Cassell, 1996) 89, emphasis added.

[41] David Powlison, "Which Presuppositions? Secular Psychology and the Categories of Biblical Thought," *Journal of Psychology and Theology* 12 (1984) 270–78.

[42] Browning, *Religious Thought and the Psychotherapies,* 241.

[43] James Loder, *The Transforming Moment,* 28, n. 7. "Interest" is a technical term of Jürgen Habermas's with the connotation of "vested."

able insights. "No philosopher has succeeded in being a consistent rationalist, empiricist, or subjectivist, though . . . Parmenides came close to being a consistent rationalist, John Stuart Mill a consistent empiricist, and Protagoras and other Sophists consistent subjectivists."[44] More frequently a rationalistic philosophy includes subjectivist elements. For instance, Kant's philosophy (1724–1804) set up the division of two realms, a "phenomenal," where reason reigns supreme and a "noumenal" where nothing can be humanly known. Descartes, Spinoza, and Leibniz worked out rationalistic systems but on subjectivistic bases. Locke, Berkeley, and Hume worked out subjectivistic systems on rationalistic bases. The rational impulse and the subjectivistic impulse operate dialectically within the greatest philosophical systems.[45]

A similar oscillation to the philosophical dialectic of rational and subjective appears in theology. In this perspective, H. Richard Niebuhr's *Christ and Culture* is a typology of cultural expressions of immanence alternating with expressions of transcendence. The oscillation reappears when immanentistic nineteenth-century liberalism gave way from the 1920s to the transcendentally oriented theology of Karl Barth. Like the rationalist-irrationalist dialectic in philosophy, the immanent-transcendent issue has long roots in the Christian tradition. The second-century theologian Tertullian famously asked, "What has Jerusalem to do with Athens?"[46] What has divine revelation to do with profane reason? Yet at nearly the same time, Clement of Alexandria wrote, "Some, who think themselves naturally gifted, do not wish to touch either philosophy or logic; nay more, they do not wish to learn natural science. They demand bare faith alone, as if they wished, without bestowing any care on the vine, straightway to gather clusters from the first."[47]

Immanent or at least other-than-Christian thinking was controversial in the church from the earliest time. The bishop responsible for the University of Paris, an Augustinian institution, in 1277 proscribed

---

[44] John M. Frame, *Doctrine of the Knowledge of God* (Phillipsburg, N.J.: Presbyterian and Reformed Publishing, 1989) 110.

[45] Frame, *Cornelius Van Til: An Analysis of His Thought* (Phillipsburg, N.J.: Presbyterian and Reformed Publishing, 1995) 235.

[46] H. I. Marrou, *A History of Education in Antiquity*, trans. George Lamb (Madison: University of Wisconsin Press, 1982) 315–20.

[47] Edward J. Power, *Main Currents in the History of Education* (New York: McGraw-Hill, 1962) 173. Similar is Clement in *Stromateis* VI.9: "Philosophy . . . is . . . making ready the way for him who is being perfected in Christ." In H. V. Gwatkin, *Selections from Early Writers* (London: Clarke, 1958) 106. Clement's view prevailed in e.g. theological education—the liberal arts's B.A. precedes theological education's M.Div. or M.Th.

the thought of Aristotle as mediated by the Muslim scholar Averroës.[48] Thomas Aquinas's synthesis of Augustine and Aristotle, which came from the controversy, provided a basis for centuries of Catholic theology and ecclesiology.[49]

Lee's macrotheory proposal raises a basic problem in religious educating. Do we educate by sight alone or by faith alone? Or by faith informed but not dictated by sight? Lee wishes to educate by reason, not by faith. No one would wish not to be reasonable. The problem is the grounds of reason.

Asking for a bridge between objectivity and subjectivity is to ask for an escape from the dilemma. The deficits of objective knowing or, alternately, subjective knowing, are there to be seen. Is a bridge of the immanent-transcendent divide possible? Is sure knowledge humanly possible?

A Narrative Bridge

An alternative to Thomist or modernist bridges is a narrative bridge. Narrative can link immanence to transcendence.

Historically, a way of reconciling transcendent with immanent data is Aquinas's nature-grace schema. Grace does not negate nature but perfects it; or, to rephrase the familiar formula, transcendence does not negate immanence but perfects it. Profiling this theology, Hendrikus Berkhof says that Thomistic theology had potential to do more yet—to bridge Christian faith and the modern world. This potential arose from the way that Thomism "proceeds from the assumption of harmony between nature and grace...."[50] That potential, however, went largely unfulfilled. Berkhof says this is due to intransigence by church authorities. The intransigence was due again to Rome being comparatively sheltered from the challenge of secular thought to which Northern European thinkers were fully exposed. Accordingly, Dutch, Belgian, French and German authors were willing to face the challenge of secular thinking and to restate theology in a new mode.

---

[48] Discussion in McGiffert, *History of Christian Thought*, 257–58; Jaroslav Pelikan, *The Christian Tradition*, Vol. 3: *The Growth of Medieval Theology (600–1300)* (Chicago: University of Chicago Press, 1978) 289–90.

[49] MacIntyre, *Three Rival Versions of Moral Inquiry*, 130–43.

[50] He continues, "One might think that Thomas's adage...could have been made fruitful again...over against the challenge of Enlightenment thought." Berkhof, *Two Hundred Years*, 229.

Berkhof's assessment is mirrored within Lee's writing. Berkhof's section "Immanent Transcendentality" profiles twentieth century Catholic modernist theologians. These include Maurice Blondel, Henri de Lubac, Karl Rahner, and others. These theologians theorized in the shadow of *Pascendi dominici gregis,* the encyclical of 1907 that condemned immanentist theology and which was periodically reinforced.[51] Not until Vatican II would the shadow lift. In general, the modern Catholic approach has accented immanence much more strongly than transcendence. Rahner's theology walks carefully and with great sophistication on the edge of an immanentist cliff. Teilhard de Chardin, whose thought is a branch off the main stream, also represents an accentuated immanence. Teilhard was a Jesuit priest and a paleontologist and he advanced a theology of evolutionary process. His reconstructed Christ is virtually identified with the developing creation.[52] In his textbooks Lee uses the immanentist theology. A great gulf is set up between a transcendent God and the immanent alternative.[53] For Lee, the social sciences are no longer "godless" or "atheistic." He is in harmony with the dominant immanentism. There seems to be no middle way.

In his way, Teilhard appears to recognize the central place for narrative by the speaking of a "cosmic Christ." But Teilhard's Christ is abstract, timeless. He is in every aspect of the creation, at all times, in every situation, and may never be evaded. The particularistic narrative about Jesus of Nazareth is nearly unnecessary to Teilhard's construction. "Christ" usually is a subject in stories that define him. Reconciliations of transcendence with immanence are too often abstract. The reconciliations come in philosophical language lacking any historical context. They are speculative, to borrow a term from Lee.

A Van Til-type alternative to a timeless reconciliation runs as follows. Let us affirm that any construction of the world is a construction of faith. The question of faiths is a worldview question. Worldviews are mediated by narratives. Some narratives encompass reality in more adequate fashion than others. Some narratives underwrite life more fully.

A narrative mediating a worldview is found in the New Testament.[54] Viewing canonical statements as propositions only is a mistake. Theological

---

[51] Boys, *Educating in Faith*, 89; Berkhof, 235–36.

[52] Berkhof, *Two Hundred Years*, 229–55; Grenz and Olsen, *Twentieth-Century Theology*, 237–70; J.J. Duyvené de Wit, "Pierre Teilhard de Chardin," 407–50; Teilhard de Chardin, *Hymn of the Universe*, trans. Gerald Vann (New York: Harper & Row, 1965).

[53] e.g. Lee, *Principles of Secondary Education*, 61–62; *Purpose*, 11, 42.

[54] N. T. Wright, *Christian Origins and the Question of God*, Vol. 1: *The New Testament and*

propositions are not isolated individual statements. They are coherent in a system. Theological or biblical propositions are apprehended by faith. The fact that story articulates a worldview accounts for the reason disputes in that field can be fierce: not just an exegetical account is at stake but an element is at play between one worldview and another. John Milbank, the critic of social theory, and N. T. Wright, a notable New Testament scholar, affirm a central role for worldview. Narrative bridges contingency and general theory.[55] That is, narrative links historical particularity to the big picture.

The New Testament narrative identifies and defines Christ. Jesus' presence is immanent; Jesus is truly human. His presence is also transcendent. He is truly God.[56] Immanence and transcendence are held together in the narrative of creation, fall, and redemption. Christ reveals ultimate reality in unique fashion.[57] Person and words both serve to reveal God. Like his person, Jesus' words are incarnational. Like the person, the recorded revelation is identifiable across cultures, able to redeem them, and able to provide a standard of judgment. The revelation is not limited by human verbal, cultural constructions but is able to speak within them. Is this a matter of faith? Yes. And in classical style, this faith becomes the basis for genuine rationality.[58] Subject and object are united in Christ.

Because humanity shares life in God's created order, worldviews are not incommensurable. Translation, though imperfect, is possible. We may compare our beliefs in humane fashion. By the same coin, no worldview is timeless, a-cultural, or a-historical.[59] The Christian system always needs to be restated for a new cultural situation.[60]

---

the People of God (Minneapolis: Fortress, 1992) 65. Wright sets out a prolegomena for a three-volume New Testament theology, 29–144.

[55] Milbank, *Theology and Social Theory*, 70–71.

[56] The two sides are epitomized in the statement at Romans 1:1-2.

[57] John's gospel highlights Jesus as himself revelatory: 1:18; 5:37; 6:46; 8:38; 14:7, 9; 15:24.

[58] Augustine is credited with the first version of Anselm of Canterbury's *credo ut intelligam*—"I believe in order than I might understand." In this perspective learning is faith seeking understanding.

[59] Brian J. Walsh, "Transformation: Dynamic Worldview or Repressive Ideology?," *Journal of Education and Christian Belief* 4 (2000) 228–48. There is a large literature on contextualization. See Harvie Conn, *Eternal Word and Changing Worlds: Theology, Anthropology, and Mission in Trialogue* (Grand Rapids: Zondervan, 1984); or David J. Bosch, *Transforming Mission: Paradigm Shifts in Theology of Mission* (Mary-knoll, N.Y.: Orbis, 1996).

[60] N. T. Wright, "The Book and the Story," *Bible in Transmission* (Summer 1997) has an expanded worldview account of Christian faith similar to that in this paragraph. Retrieved

Christian living is held together in a personal narrative of creation, fall, and redemption. The redemption is both finalized in principle, and an ongoing process. We are in process and the process is painful. In this perspective genuine Christian education will not rhyme off the mechanics but introduce learners to the dynamic of living in faith.Learners will learn to see themselves as active players in the narrative.

The realization of the pervasiveness of worldview is pertinent to our consideration of Lee's social science religious instruction proposal. The New Testament narrative proposal contrasts with Lee's immanentist, subjectivist proposal. The issue is significant because education theory humanizes or dehumanizes based on its implicit view of the human person.

Empiricism Again

Recognizing the worldview rootedness of comparative empirical study does not negate quantitative measures. There continues to be a place for empirical study. Empirical study makes definite contributions. But it must be understood as importing the assumptions of an observer. Educators should not intend to take their eyes out. My argument is that theorists should work out the "armchair" prolegomena first, and only then seek numerical measures. Empirical facts are metaphysically committed. Karl Mannheim predicted years ago that sociology might have to pass through a naive empirical phase as did psychology.[61] Not to acknowledge one's presuppositions is to lose flexibility.[62] John Milbank appears to agree. Initially he seemed to want to displace secular social theory altogether. More recently he affirms that he wants "to free (empirical observation) from a questionable metaphysical framework" and thus to clear the way for the generation of more solid numbers.[63] The social sciences mediate metaphysical understandings to the level of practice. Lee's career of advocacy might have served to make an opening to an important methodological consideration for religious instruction.

Lee's work bears a degree of persuasion because he is right that the "natural" (as opposed to the supernatural) cannot be neglected. Theologically committed educators balk, however, at the implication that

---

from <http://biblesociety.org.uk> on March 12, 2004.

[61] Mannheim, "Theology and the Sociology of Knowledge," 84.

[62] Ibid., 90.

[63] "Theology and Social Theory and Its Significance for Community Building: A Conversation with John Milbank," Theology and Community Building Workgroup seminar, Charlottesville, Va., December 16, 2000, retrieved from <http://www.livedtheology.org> on March 6, 2004.

spiritual work is finally human work. We are religious educators. In religious education, of all places, human effort cannot be the decisive factor. Maybe the resistance that Lee encountered to his theory is a kind of last stand. Christian or religious education might be one location where it has to be recognized that humans do not arrange God. God arranges us. The response to preaching and teaching is never programmable. There is cognitive knowledge on one hand, and then knowledge in love. Cognition can only come alive by the unaccountable Spirit.

Lee's stated problem is theology's inapplicability.[64] Lee wants a faith that works. While God does indeed work through immanent means, he cannot be compelled. The immanent working of God is the subject of centuries of theological discussion. All major systems must deal with it. One answer as to the link between human work and God's work, our faith and God's reply comes, again, from Dietrich Bonhoeffer. You cannot make yourself have faith, but you can come and hear the message. You will not respond in faith if you do not come to hear.[65] The "means of grace" is a phrase expressing a paradox: the work is human but the action is prescribed by God and to be vital requires his action.

Educators must know what they are doing. A field must have definite methodologies that shape its products. Certain ideas will control the selection of other ideas. Ideas of the ideal human being in an ideal society social setting—inherent in a worldview—will govern the development of the theory and the selection of components.

Is a macro-theory possible? The particularity of educational theory means that no macro-theory for all religions is possible. Assumptions about, for example, truly human existence are varied. But dialogue, the practical exercise of worldview comparison, remains highly valuable. Religious education is an interdisciplinary meeting place where disciplines contribute to meet a practical need.

My thesis reinforces the thrust of Mary Boys's *Educating in Faith*. All education is theologically specific, rooted, dependent on a paradigm. An educational system is a child of its historical-theological-philosophical circumstances. Thus, an unexamined metaphysics roots Lee's social science religious instruction proposal. Assumptions to do with the nature of persons, the church, or society—always inherent in empirical data—may no longer be taken over uncritically with the data.

---

[64] Lee, *Flow*, 218; O'Hare, "Image of Theology," 458.

[65] Bonhoeffer, *Cost of Discipleship*, 70.

Randolph Crump Miller admitted long ago, "[W]e still have not discovered how to make the truths of the Christian Gospel relevant to everyday living in terms which can be observed."[66] The current need in religious educational methodology is a linkage for theology and Christian practice. Theologies must carry applications with them. The most basic theological understandings—of God, humanity, the church, and society—must be mediated into practices consistent with those understandings. In the wake of reflection on the theology-social science relationship, an understanding of the human being that can only be termed "theological" will have to be employed for consistent religious education. James Michael Lee's empirical religious education theory points beyond itself, to the need for worldview to be recognized as inherent in any practice of education.

---

[66] Randolph Crump Miller, *The Clue to Christian Education* (New York: Scribner, 1950) 17.

Bibliography

Adorno, Theodor W. et. al. *The Positivist Dispute in German Sociology.* Translated by Glyn Adey and David Frisby. New York: Harper & Row, 1976.
Allen, R. T. "The Philosophy of Michael Polanyi and Its Significance for Education." *Journal of Philosophy of Education* 12 (1978) 167–77.
Anderson, Ray S. *On Being Human: Essays in Theological Anthropology.* Grand Rapids: Eerdmans, 1982.
Anthony, Michael J., editor. *Evangelical Dictionary of Christian Education.* Grand Rapids: Baker, 2001.
Audi, Robert, general editor. *Cambridge Dictionary of Philosophy.* 2d ed. Cambridge: Cambridge University Press, 1999.
Baatuma, Wilson Ssekandi. "An Integrative Approach to Teaching-Learning Processes Derived from the Theories of Randolph Crump Miller and James Michael Lee." Ed. D. diss., Southern Baptist Theological Seminary, 1986.
Barnes, Michael Horace, editor. *Theology and the Social Sciences.* Maryknoll, N.Y.: Orbis, 2001.
Bartolome, L. A. "Beyond the Methods Fetish: Toward a Humanizing Pedagogy." *Harvard Educational Review* 64 (1994) 173–94.
Baum, Gregory. "Sociology and Theology." *Concilium* 1.1 (1974) 22–31.
———. *Religion and Alienation: A Theological Reading of Sociology.* New York: Paulist, 1975.
———. "Introduction." In *Sociology and Human Destiny: Essays on Sociology, Religion and Society,* edited by Gregory Baum, ix–xii. New York: Seabury, 1980.
———. "The Sociology of Roman Catholic Theology." In *Sociology and Theology: Alliance and Conflict,* edited by David Martin et al., 100–10. New York: St. Martin's, 1980.
———. "For and Against John Milbank." In *Essays in Critical Theology,* edited by Gregory Baum, 100–10. Kansas City: Sheed & Ward, 1994.
———. "Remarks of a Theologian in Dialogue with Sociology." In *Theology and the Social Sciences,* ed. Michael Horace Barnes, 3–11. Maryknoll, N.Y.: Orbis, 2001.
Berding, Joop W. A. *John Dewey's Participatory Philosophy of Education: Education, Experience and Curriculum.* Leiden: DWSO, 1999.
Blocher, Henri. *Original Sin: Illuminating the Riddle.* Grand Rapids: Eerdmans, 1997.
Bonhoeffer, Dietrich. *The Cost of Discipleship.* Translated by Reginald H. Fuller. New York: Macmillan, 1963.
Bloor, David. *Knowledge and Social Imagery.* London: Routledge and Kegan Paul, 1976.
Boys, Mary C. *Biblical Interpretation in Religious Education.* Birmingham, Ala: Religious Education Press, 1980.
———. "Curriculum Thinking from a Roman Catholic Perspective." *Religious Education* 75 (1980) 516–27.

———. "Conversion as a Foundation of Religious Education." *Religious Education* 77 (1982) 211–24.
———. "The Role of Theology in Religious Education." *Horizons* 11.1 (1984) 61–85.
———. "Teaching: the Heart of Religious Education." *Religious Education* 79 (1984) 252–72.
———. *Educating in Faith: Maps and Visions*. Kansas City: Sheed & Ward, 1989.
———. "Kerygmatic Theology and Religious Education." In *Theologies of Religious Education*, edited by Randolph Crump Miller, 230–54. Birmingham, Ala: Religious Education Press, 1995.
Browning, Don. *Religious Thought and the Modern Psychotherapies: A Critical Conversation*. Philadelphia: Fortress, 1987.
———. *A Fundamental Practical Theology*. Minneapolis: Fortress, 1991.
———. "Toward a Fundamental and Strategic Practical Theology." In *Shifting Boundaries: Contextual Approaches to the Structure of Theological Education*, edited by Barbara G. Wheeler and Edward Farley, 295–328. Louisville: Westminster John Knox, 1991.
Bryant, Christopher G. A. *Positivism in Social Theory and Research*. Basingstoke, Eng.: Macmillan, 1985.
Burgess, Harold W. *An Invitation to Religious Education*. Mishawaka, Ind: Religious Education Press, 1975.
———. *Models of Religious Education: Theory and Practice in Historical and Contemporary Perspective*. Wheaton, Ill: Victor, 1996.
Capps, Walter H. *Religious Studies: The Making of a Discipline*. Minneapolis: Fortress, 1995.
Chadwick, Henry. *Augustine*. Past Masters. Oxford: Oxford University Press, 1986.
Clark, Gordon. *From Thales to Dewey*. Jefferson, Md.: Trinity Foundation, 1985.
Copleston, F. C. *Aquinas*. Harmondsworth, Eng.: Penguin, 1955.
Coughlin, Kevin J. "Religious Education in Everyday Life." Ph.D. diss., Graduate Theological Union, 1981.
Cully, Iris, and Kendig Brubaker Cully, editors. *Process and Relationship: Issues in Theory, Philosophy, and Religious Education*. Birmingham, Ala.: Religious Education Press, 1978.
Descartes, René. *A Discourse on Method*. Introduction by A. D. Lindsay. Translated by John Veitch. New York: Dutton, 1912.
Duchesne, Louis. *Early History of the Christian Church: From Its Foundation to the End of the Fifth Century*. Vol. 3: *The Fifth Century*. Translated by C. Jenkins. London: John Murray, 1924.
Dunne, Joseph. *Back to the Rough Ground: Practical Judgment and the Lure of Technique*. Notre Dame: University of Notre Dame Press, 1993.
Eisner, Elliott. *The Educational Imagination*. New York: Macmillan, 1979.
Evans, C. S. *Preserving the Person: A Look at Human Sciences*. Downers Grove, Ill: InterVarsity, 1977.
Falbo, Mark Charles. "Theory and Praxis of Conversion in the Religious Education of Non-Poor Youth: An Educational Analysis of Bernard Lonergan on Conversion and Paulo Freire on Conscientization." Ph.D. diss., Boston College, 1991.
Ferris, Nancy Kraft. "Nurturing Social Consciousness Through Church Education." Ph.D. diss., University of Pittsburgh, 1992.
Fernhout, Harry. "Where is Faith?" In *Faith Development and Fowler*, edited by Craig Dykstra and Sharon Parks, 71–87. Birmingham, Ala: Religious Education Press, 1986.

Feyerabend, Paul. *Against Method: Outline of an Anarchistic Theory of Knowledge.* London: NLB, 1975.
Fiorenza, Francis Schüssler. *Foundational Theology: Jesus and the Church.* New York: Crossroad, 1984.
Fowler, H. W., and F. G. Fowler. *Oxford Concise Dictionary of Current English.* 5th ed. Revised by E. McIntosh. Oxford: Oxford University Press, 1964.
Frame, John M. *Doctrine of the Knowledge of God.* Phillipsburg, N.J.: Presbyterian and Reformed Publishing, 1989.
———. *Cornelius Van Til: An Analysis of His Thought.* Phillipsburg, N.J.: Presbyterian and Reformed Publishing, 1995.
Freedman, David Noel, editor. *Eerdmans Dictionary of the Bible.* Grand Rapids: Eerdmans, 2000.
Gadamer, Hans-Georg: *Truth and Method.* 2d ed. Translated by J. Weinsheimer and D. Marshall. New York and London: Continuum, 1989.
Gay, Craig. "Evangelicals and the Language of Technopoly." *Crux* 31.1 (1995) 32–40.
Giannetti, Eduardo. *Lies We Live By: The Art of Self-Deception.* London: Bloomsbury, 2001.
Giddens, Anthony. *Modernity and Self-Identity: Self and Society in the Late Modern Age.* Stanford, Calif.: Stanford University Press, 1991.
Gill, Robin, editor. *Theology and Sociology: A Reader.* Enlarged ed. London: Cassell, 1996.
Glen, J. Stanley. *The Recovery of the Teaching Ministry.* Philadelphia: Westminster, 1960.
Gouldner, Alvin. *Enter Plato: Classical Greece and the Origins of Social Theory.* New York: Basic Books, 1965.
Grenz, Stanley J., and Roger E. Olsen. *Twentieth-Century Theology: God and the World in a Transitional Age.* Downers Grove, Ill: InterVarsity, 1992.
Grimes, Howard. Review of *The Flow of Religious Instruction,* by James Michael Lee. *Perkins Journal* 27 (1974) 58–59.
———. "Theological Foundations for Christian Education." In *An Introduction to Christian Education,* edited by Marvin J. Taylor, 32–41. Nashville: Abingdon, 1966.
Groome, Thomas. *Christian Religious Education: Sharing Our Story and Vision.* San Francisco: Harper & Row, 1980.
Hanson, N. R. *Patterns of Discovery: An Inquiry into the Conceptual Foundations of Science.* Cambridge: Cambridge University Press, 1958.
Harding, Sandra. *The Science Question in Feminism.* Ithaca: Cornell University Press, 1986.
Hobson, Peter, and Louise Welbourne. "Modal Shifts and Challenges for Religious Education in Catholic Schools Since Vatican II." *Christian Education Journal* 6 (Spring 2002) 56.
Huebner, Dwayne. "Religious Metaphors in the Language of Education." *Religious Education* 8 (1985) 460–72.
Kincaid, Harold. *Philosophical Foundations of the Social Sciences: Analyzing Controversies in Social Research.* Cambridge: Cambridge University Press, 1996.
Knox, Ian. *Above or Within?: The Supernatural in Religious Education.* Mishawaka, Ind.: Religious Education Press, 1976.
Kolakowski, Leszek. *Positivist Philosophy: From Hume to the Vienna Circle.* Harmondworth, Eng.: Penguin, 1972.
Kuhn, Thomas S. *The Structure of Scientific Revolutions.* 2d ed. Chicago: University of Chicago Press, 1970.

Lakoff, George, and Mark Johnson. *Metaphors We Live By.* Chicago: University of Chicago Press, 1980.

Lazarsfeld, Paul F. "Philosophy of Science and Empirical Social Research." In *Logic, Methodology and the Philosophy of Science,* edited by Ernest Nagel, Patrick Suppes and Alfred Tarski, 463–73. Stanford: Stanford University Press, 1962.

Lee, James Michael. "The Place of Science in the High School Curriculum." *Catholic Educational Review* 57 (May 1959) 32–37.

———. "Professional Criticism of Catholic High Schools." *Catholic World* (October 1961) 7–12.

———. *Principles and Methods of Secondary Education.* New York: McGraw-Hill, 1963.

———. "Counseling versus Discipline: Another View." *Catholic Counselor* 7 (Spring 1963) 114–19.

———, and Louis-J. Putz, editors. *Seminary Education in a Time of Change.* Notre Dame, Ind.: Fides, 1965.

———, and Nathaniel Pallone. *Guidance and Counseling in Schools: Foundations and Processes.* New York: McGraw-Hill, 1966.

———, and Nathaniel J. Pallone, editors. *Readings in Guidance and Counseling.* New York: Sheed and Ward, 1966.

———. "The Objective of the Roman Catholic Seminary." *Theological Education* 2 (Winter 1966) 95–110.

———, editor. *Catholic Education in the Western World.* Notre Dame: University of Notre Dame Press, 1967.

———. "America's Catholic Schools." *Herder Correspondence* 4 (November 4, 1967) 319–24.

———. "Religious Education: What Is It?" *Discovery: A Forum for High School Religion Teachers* (March 1968) 1–3.

———. "Catholic Education: Winds of Change." *Ave Maria* 17 (April 13, 1968) 7–9, 29–31.

———. "The New Style of Catechetics in the USA." *Herder Correspondence* 5.5 (1968) 141–45.

———. *The Purpose of Catholic Schooling.* Washington, D.C. and Dayton, Ohio: National Catholic Education Association and Pflaum, 1968.

———, and John T. Hiltz. "Diocesan Religion Programs: A National Survey." *Catholic Educational Review* 66 (1968) 553–65.

———. "The Third Strategy: A Behavioral Approach to Religious Education." *Today's Catholic Teacher* (September 1969) 1–12, 41–47.

———. "The Thrust of the Three Strategies in Religious Education." *Today's Catholic Teacher* (October 1969) 14–19.

———. "Social Science Catechetics." *Today's Catholic Teacher* (November 1969) 22–27.

———. "American Catholic Education." In *Does the Church Know How to Teach?: An Ecumenical Inquiry,* edited by Kendig B. Cully, 3–21. New York: Macmillan, 1970.

———, and Patrick C. Rooney, editors. *Toward a Future for Religious Education.* Dayton, Ohio: Pflaum, 1970.

———. "Behavioral Objectives in Religious Education." *The Living Light* 7.4 (1970) 12–19.

———. *The Shape of Religious Education: A Social Science Approach.* Dayton, Ohio: Pflaum, 1971.

———. "Toward a Dialogue in Religious Instruction." *The Living Light* 8.1 (1971) 19–118.

———. "Prediction in Religious Education." *The Living Light* 9.2 (1972) 43–54.
———. "Hope in Instructional Practice." *Religious Education* 67 (Sept–Oct 1972) 368–374.
———. *The Flow of Religious Instruction: A Social Science Approach.* Mishawaka, Ind: Religious Education Press, 1973.
———. "Religious Education and the Catholic University." *Notre Dame Journal of Education* 4.3 (1973) 276–83.
———. "Forward Together: A Training Program for Religious Educators." Chicago: Thomas More Association, Meditape Program, 1973.
———. "Roman Catholic Religious Education." In *Foundations for Religious Education in an Era of Change,* edited by Marvin J. Taylor, 242–58. Nashville: Abingdon, 1976.
———, editor. *The Religious Education We Need: Toward The Renewal Of Christian Education.* Mishawaka, Ind: Religious Education Press, 1977.
———. "Christian Religious Education and Moral Development." In *Moral Development, Moral Education, and Kohlberg: Basic Issues in Philosophy, Psychology, Religion, and Education,* edited by Brenda Munsey, 326–355. Birmingham: Religious Education Press, 1980.
———. "Religion and Public Schools: A Pluralistic View." *California Journal of Teacher Education* 9.2 (1982) 1–30.
———. "Response to Dwayne E. Huebner." *Religious Education* 77 (July–August 1982) 383–95.
———. "The Authentic Source of Religious Instruction." In *Religious Education and Theology,* edited by Norma H. Thompson, 100–97. Birmingham, Ala: Religious Education Press, 1982.
———. "To Basically Change Fundamental Theory and Practice." In *Modern Masters of Religious Education,* edited by Marlene Mayr, 254–323. Birmingham, Ala: Religious Education Press, 1983.
———. "Religious Education and the Bible: A Religious Educationist's View." In *Biblical Themes in Religious Education,* edited by Joseph S. Marino, 1–61. Birmingham, Ala: Religious Education Press, 1983.
———. "John Dewey and the Unification Church: Some Points of Contact." In *Unity in Diversity,* edited by Henry O. Thompson, 371–93. New York: Rose of Sharon, 1984.
———. *The Content of Religious Instruction: A Social Science Approach.* Birmingham, Ala: Religious Education Press, 1985.
———, editor. *The Spirituality of the Religious Educator.* Birmingham, Ala: Religious Education Press, 1985.
———. "CCD Renewal." In *Renewing the Sunday School and the CCD,* edited by D. Campbell Wyckoff, 211–44. Birmingham, Ala: Religious Education Press, 1986.
———. "Catechesis Sometimes, Religious Instruction Always: Another Roman Catholic Perspective." In *Does the Church Really Want Religious Education?,* edited by Marlene Mayr, 32–66. Birmingham, Ala: Religious Education Press, 1988.
———. "Social Science." In *Harper's Encyclopedia of Religious Education,* edited by Iris V. Cully and Kendig B. Cully. New York: Harper and Row, 1990.
———, editor. *Handbook of Faith.* Birmingham, Ala: Religious Education Press, 1990.
———. "Compassion in Religious Instruction." In *Compassionate Ministry,* edited by Gary L. Sapp, 171–216. Birmingham, Ala: Religious Education Pr, 1993.
———. "Publisher's Introduction." In *Theologies of Religious Education,* edited by R. C. Miller, 1–4. Birmingham, Ala.: Religious Education Press, 1995.

———. "Religious Instruction and Religious Experience." In *Handbook of Religious Experience,* edited by Ralph W. Hood, 535–67. Birmingham, Ala: Religious Education Press, 1995.

———. "The Social-Science Approach To Religious Instruction" [videorecording]. Birmingham, Ala: Religious Education Press, 1999.

———. *The Sacrament of Teaching: A Social Science Approach.* Birmingham, Ala.: Religious Education Press, 1999.

———, editor. *Forging a Better Religious Education in the Third Millennium.* Birmingham, Ala: Religious Education Press, 2001.

Little, Sara. "Belief and Behavior." *Religious Education* 73 (1978) 398–409.

———. "Theology and Religious Education." In *Foundations for Christian Education in an Era of Change,* edited by Marvin J. Taylor, 31–35. Nashville: Abingdon, 1976.

———. "Theology and Education." In *Harper's Encyclopedia of Religious Education,* edited by Iris V. Cully and Kendig B. Cully. New York: Harper & Row, 1990.

———. "The 'Clue' to Religious Education." *Union Seminary Quarterly Review* 47.2 (1993) 7–21.

Lindbeck, George. *The Nature of Doctrine: Religion and Theology in a Postliberal Age.* Philadelphia: Fortress, 1983.

Loder, James. "Sociocultural Foundations for Christian Education." In *An Introduction to Christian Education,* edited by Marvin J. Taylor, 71–84. Nashville: Abingdon, 1966.

———. *The Transforming Moment: Understanding Convictional Experiences.* San Francisco: Harper & Row, 1981.

———. "Theology and Psychology." In *Dictionary of Pastoral Care and Counseling,* edited by Rodney J. Hunter et. al. Nashville: Abingdon, 1990.

———. *The Logic of the Spirit.* San Francisco: Jossey-Bass, 1998.

MacIntyre, Alasdair C. *Three Rival Versions of Moral Enquiry: Encyclopaedia, Genealogy, and Tradition: Being Gifford Lectures delivered in the University of Edinburgh in 1988.* London: Duckworth, 1990.

Mager, Robert F. *Preparing Instructional Objectives.* Palo Alto, Calif: Fearon, 1962.

Marrou, H. I. *A History of Education in Antiquity.* Translated by George Lamb. Madison: University of Wisconsin Press, 1982.

Marthaler, Berard. "Discipline in Search of an Identity: Religious Education." *Horizons* 3 (1976) 205–9.

Martin, Robert K. *The Incarnate Ground of Christian Faith: Toward a Christian Theological Epistemology for the Educational Ministry of the Church.* Lanham, Md.: University Press of America, 1998.

McBrien, Richard P. "Toward an American Catechesis." *The Living Light* 13.2 (1976) 167–81.

McGiffert, A. C. *A History of Christian Thought.* Vol. 2: *The West from Tertullian to Erasmus.* New York: Scribners, 1933.

Mele, Alfred R. *Self-Deception Unmasked.* Princeton: Princeton University Press, 2001.

Moore, Mary Elizabeth Mullino. *Teaching from the Heart: Theology and Educational Method.* Minneapolis: Fortress, 1991.

Merry, Michael. "Social Science Theory in Religious Education According to James Michael Lee: Considerations for the Orthodox." *Saint Vladimir's Theological Quarterly* 44 (2000) 83–102.

Milbank, John. *Theology and Social Theory: Beyond Secular Reason.* Oxford: Blackwell, 1991.

———. "Theology and Social Theory and Its Significance for Community Building: A Conversation with John Milbank." Transcript of Theology and Community Building Workgroup seminar, Charlottesville, Virginia, December 16, 2000. Retrieved from www.livedtheology.org, Nov. 1, 2001.

Miller, R. C. *The Clue to Christian Education.* New York: Scribners, 1950.

———. "Some Clarifying Thoughts about Religious Education." *The Living Light* 13.4 (1976) 495.

———. *The Theory of Religious Education Practice.* Birmingham, Ala: Religious Education Press, 1980.

———. "Theology in the Background." In *Religious Education and Theology*, edited by Norma H. Thompson, 17–41. Birmingham, Ala: Religious Education Press, 1982.

Moran, Gabriel. "Two Languages of Religious Education." *The Living Light* 14.1 (1977) 7.

———. "From Obstacle to Modest Contributor: Theology in Religious Education." In *Religious Education and Theology*, edited by Norma H. Thompson, 42–47. Birmingham, Ala: Religious Education Press, 1982.

Mulkay, Michael. *Science and the Sociology of Knowledge.* London: George Allen & Unwin, 1979.

Murphey, Murray G. "On the Scientific Study of Religion in the United States, 1870–1980." In *Religion and Twentieth-Century American Intellectual Life,* edited by Michael J. Lacey, 136–70. Cambridge: Cambridge University Press, 1989.

Murray, Eileen. "Religious Education: Theological or Social Science?" *Bangalore Theological Forum* 19 (January–April 1987) 33–47.

Nelson, C. Ellis. "Protestant Church Instruction." In *Toward a Future for Religious Education,* edited by James Michael Lee and Patrick C. Rooney, 154–81. Dayton, Ohio: Pflaum, 1970.

———. Review of *The Flow of Religious Instruction* by James Michael Lee. *The Living Light* 11.1 (1974) 146–48.

Niebuhr, H. Richard. *Christ and Culture.* New York: Harper & Brothers, 1951.

Noll, Mark. "Traditional Christianity and the Possibility of Historical Knowledge." *Christian Scholar's Review* 19 (1990) 388–406.

O'Hare, Padraic. "The Image of Theology in the Educational Theory of James Michael Lee." *The Living Light* 11 (1974) 452–458.

———, editor. *Foundations of Religious Education.* New York: Paulist, 1978.

Olthuis, James H. "On Worldviews." *Christian Scholar's Review* 14 (1985) 153–64.

O'Neill, Michael. Review of *The Shape of Religious Instruction* by James Michael Lee. *The Living Light* 9.1 (1972) 143–45.

Ong, Walter. *Ramus: Method, and the Decay of Dialogue: From the Art of Discourse to the Art of Reason.* Cambridge: Harvard University Press, 1958.

Osmer, Richard. "Rationality in Practical Theology: A Map of the Emerging Discussion." *International Journal of Practical Theology* 1 (1997) 11–40.

Osterman, Mary Jo, Fern K. Willets, and A. Duncan Yokum. "The Two Hundred Year Struggle for Protestant Religious Education Curriculum Theory." *Religious Education* 75 (1980) 528–38.

Palmer, Parker J. *To Know as We Are Known: A Spirituality of Education.* San Francisco: Harper & Row, 1983.

Pannenberg, Wolfhart. *Anthropology in Theological Perspective.* Translated by Matthew J. O'Connell. Philadelphia: Westminster, 1985.

Phenix, Philip H. *Religious Concerns in Contemporary Education.* New York: Bureau of Publications, Teachers College, Columbia University, 1959.

———. *Education and the Worship of God.* Philadelphia: Westminster, 1966.

Pelikan, Jaroslav. *The Christian Tradition.* Vol. 1: *The Emergence of the Catholic Tradition, 100–600.* Chicago: University of Chicago Press, 1971.

Phillips, D. C., and Nicholas C. Burbules. *Postpositivism and Educational Research.* Lanham, Md.: Rowman and Littlefield, 2000.

Plantinga, Cornelius. *Not the Way It's Supposed to Be: A Breviary of Sin.* Grand Rapids: Eerdmans, 1994.

Polanyi, Michael. *Personal Knowledge: Toward a Post-Critical Philosophy.* Chicago: University of Chicago Press, 1958.

Poochigian, Ruth L. "A Critical Analysis of Selected Roman Catholic Religious Education Theorists from the Perspective of Adult Education Research and Theory." Ph.D. diss., University of Wisconsin, Madison, 1986.

Power, Edward J. *Main Currents in the History of Education.* New York: McGraw-Hill, 1962.

Powlison, David A. "Which Presuppositions? Secular Psychology and the Categories of Biblical Thought." *Journal of Psychology and Theology* 12 (1984) 270–78.

Poythress, Vern S. *Science and Hermeneutics.* Foundations of Contemporary Interpretation 6. Grand Rapids: Zondervan, 1988.

Proctor, Robert N. *Value-Free Science?: Purity and Power in Modern Knowledge.* Cambridge: Harvard University Press, 1991.

Quine, W. V. "Two Dogmas of Empiricism." In *A Logical Point of View,* 20–46. Cambridge: Harvard University Press, 1981. Retrieved from <http://www.ditext.com/quine/quine.html>.

Radnitzky, Gerard. *Contemporary Schools of Metascience.* 2d rev. ed. Vol. 1: *Anglo-Saxon Schools of Metascience.* Göteborg: Scandinavian University Books, [1968] 1970.

Reuben, Julie A. *The Making of the Modern University: Intellectual Transformation and the Marginalization of Morality.* Chicago: University of Chicago Press, 1996.

Ross, Dorothy. "The Development of the Social Sciences." In *The Organization of Knowledge in Modern America, 1860–1920,* edited by Alexandra Oleson and John Voss, 100–10. Baltimore: Johns Hopkins University Press, 1979.

Rothstein, Edward. "Coming to Blows Over How Valid Science Really Is." *New York Times* (July 21, 2001) B9.

Schwehn, Mark R. *Exiles from Eden.* New York: Oxford University Press, 1993.

Seljak, David. "Some Critical Questions for Paul Bramadat's *The Church on the World's Turf.*" Retrieved from <http://www3.sympatico.ca/ian.ritchie/SeljakonBramadat.html> on Nov. 11, 2001.

Seymour, Jack L. "Contemporary Approaches to Christian Education." *Chicago Theological Seminary Register* 69 (Spring 1979) 1–10. Reprinted in *Theological Perspectives on Christian Formation,* edited by Jeff Astley, Leslie J. Francis, and Colin Crowder, 3–13. Grand Rapids: Eerdmans, 1996.

———, and Donald E. Miller. *Contemporary Approaches to Christian Education.* Nashville: Abingdon, 1982.

———, editor. *Mapping Christian Education.* Nashville: Abingdon, 1997.

Smith, D. I. "Modern Language Pedagogy, Spiritual Development and Christian Faith: A Study of Their Interrelationships." Ph.D. diss., University of London, 2000.

———. "The Curious Idea of a Christian Teaching Method." Keynote Address at the Eighth Annual Conference of the North American Christian Foreign Language Association, Anderson University, Anderson, Indiana, March 25–27, 1999.

Smith, Sheldon. *Faith and Nurture*. New York: Scribners, 1941.

Stackhouse, John Jr. "An Anthropologist Bonds with a Tribe Called 'InterVarsity Christian Fellowship.'" *Books & Culture* 7.6 (2001) 22.

Sullivan, Edmund V. *A Critical Psychology: Interpretation of the Personal World*. New York: Plenum, 1984.

Thompson, Norma H. "Current Issues in Religious Education." *Religious Education* 73 (1978) 611–26.

———, editor. *Religious Education and Theology*. Birmingham, Ala: Religious Education Press, 1982.

Troeltsch, Ernst. *The Social Teaching of the Christian Churches*. 2 vols. Translated by Olive Wyon. London: George Allen & Unwin, 1931.

Tyler, Ralph W. *Basic Principles of Curriculum and Instruction*. Chicago: University of Chicago Press, 1949.

Van der Ven, Johannes A. *Practical Theology: An Empirical Approach*. Kampen: Kok Pharos, 1993.

Van Leeuwen, Mary Stewart. "Psychology's 'Two Cultures': A Christian Analysis." *Christian Scholar's Review* 17 (1988) 406–24.

Van Til, Cornelius. *Essays in Christian Education*. Phillipsburg: Presbyterian and Reformed, 1977.

Walsh, Brian J. Walsh, "Transformation: Dynamic Worldview or Repressive Ideology?" *Journal of Education and Christian Belief* 4.2 (2000) 228–48.

Warren, Michael. "All Contributions Cheerfully Accepted: Reflections on James Michael Lee." *The Living Light* 7.4 (1970) 2–39.

Weinsheimer, J. C. *Gadamer's Hermeneutics: A Reading of Truth and Method*. New Haven: Yale University Press, 1985.

Wilhoit, Jim. "The Impact of the Social Sciences on Religious Education." *Religious Education* 79 (1984) 367–75.

———. "The Bible Goes to Sunday School: An Historical Response to Pluralism." *Religious Education* 82 (1987) 390–404.

Winch, Peter. *The Idea of a Social Science*. London: Routledge & Kegan Paul, 1990.

Wolterstorff, Nicholas. *Divine Discourse: Philosophical Reflections on the Claim that God Speaks*. Cambridge: Cambridge University Press, 1995.

Wright, N. T. *Christian Origins and the Question of God*. Vol. 1: *The New Testament and the People of God*. Minneapolis: Fortress, 1992.

www.ingramcontent.com/pod-product-compliance
Lightning Source LLC
Chambersburg PA
CBHW072157160426
43197CB00012B/2424